James Roderick O'Flanagan

Annals, anecdotes, traits, and traditions of the Irish parliaments,

1172 to 1800

James Roderick O'Flanagan

Annals, anecdotes, traits, and traditions of the Irish parliaments, 1172 to 1800

ISBN/EAN: 9783337114947

Printed in Europe, USA, Canada, Australia, Japan

Cover: Foto ©ninafisch / pixelio.de

More available books at **www.hansebooks.com**

ANNALS, ANECDOTES, TRAITS, AND TRADITIONS OF THE IRISH PARLIAMENTS

ANNALS, ANECDOTES, TRAITS, AND TRADITIONS

OF THE

IRISH PARLIAMENTS,

1172 TO 1800.

BY

J. RODERICK O'FLANAGAN, B.L.,
AUTHOR OF
"LIVES OF THE LORD CHANCELLORS OF IRELAND,"
"THE IRISH BAR," "MUNSTER CIRCUIT,"
ETC. ETC.

DUBLIN:
M. H. GILL AND SON,
50 UPPER O'CONNELL STREET.

𝔗𝔬 𝔱𝔥𝔢 𝔥𝔬𝔫𝔬𝔲𝔯𝔢𝔡 𝔐𝔢𝔪𝔬𝔯𝔶

OF

HENRY GRATTAN,

WHOSE LAST WORDS WERE

"KEEP KNOCKING AT THE UNION,"

THE AUTHOR

DEDICATES THIS WORK.

AVONDHU GRANGE, FERMOY.

PREFACE.

As the General Election has once more placed Mr. Gladstone as Prime Minister, and that great statesman having already shown his desire to restore to Ireland the Parliament which a combination of circumstances deprived her of at the beginning of the present century, I have endeavoured in the following pages to trace the annals of the Irish Parliaments, and to show how their independence was restricted by Poynings' Law,—again by the English statute 6 George I.,—and, having gained freedom and independence in 1782, how, in the warning words of Dr. Johnson, they were robbed by the Union. Addressing an Irishman, the sturdy English author said: "Do not make a Union with us, sir; we would unite with you only to rob you."

I desire emphatically to state that the cry of Separation is wholly untrue. That cry is raised by the party who, regarding themselves as entitled to the monopoly, which they have long possessed, of the patronage, places, and profits of all offices, seek by this cry to defeat Home Rule. So far from Separation, we claim as of right our fair share in the benefits possessed by the Empire gained by Irish as well as British statesmanship, in which my own kinsman, the Right Hon. Edmund Burke, acted no small part—an Empire increased by Irish bravery and cemented by Irish blood. We are— many of us, like me—linked to Great Britain by the dearest and nearest ties of affection and friendship, to say nothing of worldly profit and intercourse. Surely every reflecting mind must be aware that in no empire in the world do all classes possess equal liberty with that conferred by the British Constitution; and while as Irishmen we desire the right to manage our own affairs in our native Parliament, we remain loyal and faithful subjects of our Gracious Queen.

As for the other cry raised to frighten ignorant people, and for party purposes, that Home Rule means Catholic Ascendancy, it is as groundless as the bugbear of Separation. I have shown the utmost toleration prevailed in Ireland during the reigns of Queen Mary and James II., and I rejoice to say no educated and enlightened Protestant in Ireland has any fears on the subject.

The friendly intercourse between England and

Ireland has dispelled many former prejudices. This is so plain, that the result of the recent General Election has convinced the great body of the electors of Great Britain that the time has at length arrived when the affairs of Ireland may be entrusted to Irishmen, and thereby enable the members of the British Parliament to devote their time to British legislation.

In the Appendix will be found the ceremonies which took place at the openings of the Irish Parliaments, the mode of proceeding during the session, and descriptions of the Houses of Lords and Commons, with many traditions of the Irish Parliaments, which may be useful when the people of Ireland enjoy Home Rule.

Trusting that day is not remote, and the course of events may show the wisdom of the measure, I submit my work to the public.

J. RODERICK O'FLANAGAN.

Avondhu Grange, Fermoy.

CONTENTS.

PREFACE, ... vi

CHAPTER I.

1172–1275.

The Anglo-Normans settle in Ireland—Council at Cashel—Henry II. acknowledged Sovereign of Ireland—How he became popular—Government of Ireland—The Pale—Reign of Henry III.—Castle of Dublin—Mode of calling Parliaments—Absent Members fined—Anecdotes of the Bishop of Emly—Magna Charta granted—Irish to have benefit of English Law, ... 1

CHAPTER II.

1275–1478.

Wogan's Parliament—The Statute of Kilkenny—The Viceroyalty of the Duke of York—His Popularity—Birth of the Duke of Clarence in 1449—His Baptism—Claim of Independent Legislation—The Earl of Desmond—His Intimacy with Edward IV.—Rash Answer to the King—The Queen's Resolve—Earl of Worcester Viceroy—Earl of Desmond tried and executed—"The Butcher of England"—His Fate—Eulogy of Caxton, . . . 6

xii   CONTENTS.

CHAPTER III.

1478–1534.

                                                                  PAGE

State of the Anglo-Norman Colony, A.D. 1478—Rival Viceroys summon Parliament—Anecdote of Dean Cobbe—State of Religion in 1484—Lambert Simnel crowned King, 1487—Perils of Members of Parliament—Henry VII.—Viceroy Sir Edward Poynings—Mode of Proceeding in Parliament—A Bridle on the Irish Parliament—Royal Favours on Sir Edward Poynings, ... 15

CHAPTER IV.

1534–1537.

Henry VIII. Head of the Church—Dr. Brown, Archbishop of Dublin—Irish refuse to renounce the Pope—The Archbishop's Letter to Cromwell—Lord Leonard Grey, Viceroy—Catholic Ceremonies observed—Parliament in 1537—Henry VIII. made King of Ireland—Statute respecting Absentee Proprietors—Effect of that Statute, 22

CHAPTER V.

1537–1603.

Reigns of Edward VI., Queen Mary, and Queen Elizabeth—Mary's Efforts to restore the Catholic Religion—The Queen requests the Pope to send a Bull restoring England to the Catholic Faith—Parliament repeals the Statute declaring Henry VIII. Head of the Church—Cardinal Pole invested with the Pallium—Archbishop Vaughan also—Anecdote of Dean Cole, and how his Mission was thwarted—Accession of Queen Elizabeth—Forfeited Estates of the Earl of Desmond—Royal Grants to Raleigh and Spenser—Kilcolman Castle—Costume in

House of Lords and Commons—Planting the Forfeited Estates—Angry Letter from the Queen to the Archbishop of Dublin—Perrot's Parliament in 1586—Members of House of Commons—Irish Chiefs attend—Attempt to evade Poynings' Law—Viceroy applies for his Recall—Tried for High Treason—Found Guilty—Sentenced—The Queen's Clemency, ... 27

CHAPTER VI.

1603-1644.

Bolton's Statutes—Heads of Bills—Accession of James I.—Disappointed Hopes—Confiscation of Ulster—Parliament in 1613—Contest for the Speakership—Charles I. sends Earl of Strafford as Viceroy—A Parliament in 1639—Serjeant Eustace, Speaker—Strafford encouraging the Linen Industry—Pym threatens—The Commission for Defective Titles—The Galway Jury—High Sheriff dies in Prison—Lord Chancellor and others impeached—Articles of Impeachment—Their Failure—Strafford and Charles I. executed, ... 39

CHAPTER VII.

1644-1685.

Bolton's Treatise—The Catholic Confederation of Kilkenny in 1642—Cromwell in Ireland—Parliament in Chichester House—Sir Audley Mervyn, Speaker—His Speech—The Adventure Act applied to Ireland—The Confederate Army fight for King Charles I.—Forfeiture of the Estates of the Confederates—The Protestant Bishop of Cork obtains good Terms for the Cromwellians—He receives Thanks of the Lords—Court of Claims—Treasonable Plots, ... 43

CHAPTER VIII.

1685–1690.

James II. King—Visits Ireland in 1688—Summons a Parliament—The King's Speech—Titles of Statutes—Sir William Petty—Statement respecting Forfeited Estates—William III. King—English Parliament annuls Irish Statutes of King James II., ... 47

CHAPTER IX.

1690–1713.

Lord Sydney, Viceroy—Parliament in 1692—Oath excluding Catholics—Viceroy desires to maintain the Treaty of Limerick—Lord Chancellor Sir Constantine Phipps censured by the House of Commons—Defended by the House of Lords—Difference between Lord Chancellor Cox and Privy Council, ... 58

CHAPTER X.

1706–1713.

On the Mode prescribed to appoint a Lord Justice—Statute 33 Henry VIII.—Contradictory Opinions thereon—How disposed of—Parliament of 1707—The Viceroy's Conciliatory Address, ... 66

CHAPTER XI.

1713–1759.

Anecdote of Addison—Parliament in 1713—George I.—The Court of Appeal—Statute 6 George I. to bind Ireland—Effect of Statute of William III.—Depressed Irish Trade—Dean Swift's Advice—Legend of Minerva and Arachne—Wood's Coinage—The Drapier's Letters—The Irish Club—A Satire on the House of Lords, . . . 69

CHAPTER XII.

1759-1760.

Anti-Union Riot in Dublin—Peers compelled to swear against a Union—The Desire in the House—Danger of the *Commons' Journal*—Ireland to hang the Secretary—No Action by the Lord Mayor—No Riot Act in Ireland—The Viceroy calls out the Military—Humane Commander-in-Chief—Loss of Life before Mob dispersed—The King indignant—The Secretary gives a Convivial Party—Has to give an Explanation, ... 81

CHAPTER XIII.

1760-1767.

Protestant Parliamentary Patriots—Lucas, Flood, Grattan, and Burgh—Charles Lucas, born 1713, died 1771—Makes Charges in Supply of Drugs—Publishes "Pharmacomastrix"—In 1741 Lucas a Town Councillor—Corporation Question decided in favour of the Aldermen of Dublin—Sends Charter to the King with Account of the Citizens being robbed of their Rights—The Lords Justices decline to send to the King—In 1733 Lucas elected Member for the City of Dublin—Directs strict Obedience to Laws in after years O'Connell declared—In 1749 the House of Commons declares Lucas an Enemy to his Country—His Conduct when arrested—Imprisoned in Newgate—The cruel Order for his Treatment in Prison induces him to Escape—Dr. Johnson's Opinion in his Favour, . . 89

CHAPTER XIV.

1767-1791.

Henry Flood, born in 1740—Member for Kilkenny—Equals Lucas in most eminent Parliamentary Talents—Accepts Office—Anger of the People—Character of the Government—Attacks on Flood by Scott—Attorney-General's comical Description of Flood under the name of Harry Plantagenet—Dispute with Grattan—Enters the British Parliament—Return to Ireland—Death in 1791—Made a large Bequest to Trinity College, Dublin—Grattan's post-mortem Eulogy, ... 104

CHAPTER XV.

HENRY GRATTAN. BORN 1746; DIED 1820.

Born in 1746—Recorder Grattan opposed to his Son's Politics—Is disinherited—A Law Student—Encounter in Windsor Forest—Called to the Irish Bar in 1772—Member for Charlemont in 1775—Efforts for Free Trade—English Hostility to Irish Industries—By Aid of the Volunteers Irish Independence gained—Political Changes in England—Viceroys changed in Ireland—Fox's Manœuvring—Great Excitement in Dublin in April 1782—Grattan in the Front—He obtains Ireland's Freedom—Vote of £100,000 to Grattan—Accepts Half—The State of Ireland in 1798 causes him to abandon attending Parliament—The Debate on the Union—Grattan's last Appeal—The Union Act—Grattan returns to Tinnahinch—Elected to represent Dublin in the United Parliament—His Fame as an Orator—The Champion of the Roman Catholics—Death—Last Words, ... 113

CHAPTER XVI.

RIGHT HON. WALTER HUSSEY BURGH. BORN 1743; DIED 1783.

Born in 1743—Education—Called to the Irish Bar, 1768—Letter on the Impolicy of Pledging Candidates—Joins the Opposition—While Prime Serjeant sacrifices Place for Patriotism—Specimens of his Oratory—Coincidence in Language between Hussey Burgh in 1769 and Lord George Bentinck in 1846—Appointed Chief Baron of the Exchequer in 1781—Death in 1783—Public Funeral—Pension on his Family—Praise by Grattan, . . 128

CHAPTER XVII.

1792-1795.

Viceroyalty of Earl FitzWilliam—Administration of Earl FitzWilliam—Promise not to oppose the Catholic Relief Bill—In 1795, the Measure brought in by Gentleman John Beresford—Pitt complains of the Viceroy—Rumours that Lord FitzWilliam was to be recalled—Conduct of the British Government—Attempt to withhold Supplies—Lord FitzWilliam writes to Mr. Pitt—The popular Viceroy leaves Ireland—Grief for his Recall, ... 141

CHAPTER XVIII.

CHANGE OF VICEROY IN 1778—THE PROPOSED REGENCY.

Duke of Rutland Viceroy—Viceroy's Salary increased—Anecdote of a Proper Rebuke—Mr. Pitt's Letter to the Duke—Death of the Duke—His Successor the Marquis of Buckingham—Insanity of King George III.—Mr. Pitt determines to restrict the Power of the Prince of Wales as Regent—The Irish Parliament grant unlimited Power—Action of the Viceroy—Gratitude of the Prince—The Round Robin—Recall of Marquis of Buckingham—Pitt's Union Policy, ... 150

CHAPTER XIX.

1795-1798.

Viceroyalty of Marquis Camden and Marquis Cornwallis—Lord Camden Viceroy in March 1795—Triumph of the Protestant Ascendancy Party—The Beresfords—Gloomy Prospects—Conflict at the Diamond—The Irish Rebel—The French in Bantry Bay in 1796—Change of Viceroy—Expedition failed—The Landing in Killala in 1798—

Withdrawal of Nationalist Members from Parliament—Encounter at Castlebar—Defeat of the British Troops—The Viceroy marches against the French—The Surrender at Ballinamuck—The Tour of the Viceroy to procure Addresses in favour of the Union—Mr. Plunket's Statement of how the Addresses were procured, . . . 157

CHAPTER XX.

1798–1800.

Marquis Cornwallis Viceroy—His Qualification for Office—Dialogue with Mr. Howard of Corby—Ignorance of the British Ministry respecting the Irish People—City of Cork supports the Union—Rebellion of 1798—Grattan and others Absent from Parliament—On his Return attacked by Mr. Corry—Grattan's scathing Reply—On Bill for O'Donnell's Motion—The Speaker appeals to the House—Effort of the Viceroy in support of the Bill—Heart of a Popular Tumult—The Speaker puts the Question—Carried, ... 164

CHAPTER XXI.

1800.

Hopes of Popular Dissent rejected — Viceroy's Efforts to procure Public Approval—His abortive Efforts to obtain Public Approval—The Bill in the House of Commons—Startling Proposal from the Gallery — Last Sitting moved by Lord Castlereagh—Distress of the Speaker (Foster)—The Members on the Question—The Ayes have it—The Bill in the Lords—The Chancellor's Speech—Praise of the Viceroy—The Lords' Debate—The Act passed—Protest of Dissentient Peers—Intended Projects for supporting Catholic Clergy—Act of Compensation for Boroughs—Popular Hits at corrupt Members, . . 169

CONTENTS.   xix

APPENDICES.

APPENDIX I.
PAGE

The Parliament House — The Exterior — Anecdote of the Statutes — A New Order of Architecture — Interior — The Houses of Lords and Commons — Cost of Erection — Floored after the Union — Sale to the Bank of Ireland, . 179

APPENDIX II.

Parliamentary Banquets peculiar to Ireland — Peers and Members of the House of Commons join in the Revelry, 181

APPENDIX III.

Attendance of High Officials — The Ceremonies respecting the Viceroy — Conference between Lords and Commons — Royal Assent — Order in the Streets — Favourite Hours of Attendance in the House of Commons, ... 183

APPENDIX IV.

Procedure during the Session, ... 184

APPENDIX V.

Statute Rolls and Journals, ... 186

APPENDIX VI.

Insults to Statue of King William III. — Hoax on Sir Philip Crampton, Surgeon-General, ... 187

APPENDIX VII.

Troubles of Speakers, ... 188

APPENDIX VIII.

Violent Language—Amicable Duels, ... 190

APPENDIX IX.

Tried by his Peers—The Kingston Tragedy—A Romance of the Irish Peerage, ... 191

APPENDIX X.

Irish Parliamentary Wits and Humorists, ... 199

APPENDIX XI.

Tottenham in his Boots, ... 202

APPENDIX XII.

A very absent Member, ... 203

APPENDIX XIII.

Mr. Pitt's Projects—Disagreement between Parliament, . 204

ANNALS, ANECDOTES, TRAITS, AND TRADITIONS OF THE IRISH PARLIAMENTS.

CHAPTER I.

1172–1275.

The Anglo-Normans settle in Ireland—Council at Cashel—Henry II. acknowledged Sovereign of Ireland—How he became popular—Government of Ireland—The Pale—Reign of Henry III.—Castle of Dublin—Mode of calling Parliaments—Absent Members fined—Anecdote of the Bishop of Emly—Magna Charta granted—Irish to have benefit of English Law.

WHEN, in A.D. 1172, Dermot MacMorrough, who was expelled from his kingdom of Leinster for the abduction of the wife of Tiernan O'Rourke, sought the aid of Henry II. to restore him to his kingdom, he found that monarch was himself expelled, and obliged to fly to France, on account of the recent assassination of Thomas à Becket, slain on the altar of the Cathedral of Canterbury, at the instigation, as it was generally supposed, of the English King.

At length Dermot found Henry, who, unable to help, sent him to a nobleman. From the offer

Dermot made and promised what he knew Strongbow needed, spoil and deeds of arms. Dermot found the Earl of Pembroke willing, and satisfied with the offer of making the earl his heir, and giving him his daughter in marriage.

Strongbow lost no time in collecting a force, which, led by his friends, Raymond le Gros, Miles de Cogan, and others, made good their hold on Ireland. Henry himself followed in October 1172, and received the submission of the clergy and chiefs of Ireland at a council held at Cashel, presided over by Christian, Bishop of Lismore, the Pope's legate in Ireland. This caused a belief that another council was held at Lismore; but when the great assembly of the prelates and Irish chiefs met at Cashel, then a more considerable place than Lismore, I think all affairs, ecclesiastical and civil, were regulated there. The authority of the King of England was thus acknowledged.

Henry remained in Ireland, having caused a temporary palace to be built in Dublin during the winter, and as he soon found the best mode of making himself popular with the Irish chiefs was by lavish hospitality, gave grand banquets, which were well attended by Irish as well as English. A century later, when an English lord was selected as viceroy, he asked a friend well acquainted with Ireland how he could make his way with the natives. The advice was, "Keep a good cook." This plan made Henry so popular, his departure from Dublin was much regretted.

Before he left Ireland, Henry also, by statute, provided that Ireland was to be governed by a viceroy and council, and in the event of any viceroy or chief governor vacating office by death or otherwise, the principal nobles and officials of the Anglo-Norman colony were empowered to elect a successor to exercise full viceregal power and authority until the king's instructions had been received. The state officials were—Lord Marshal, Lord Constable, Seneschal, Chief Butler, and Royal Standard-bearer. The *Capitalis Justiciarius* was required to give hostages for his fidelity, and directed to take the advice of the lords of the colony as Privy Councillors.[1]

At first only the English colonists, and such of the native Irish as dwelt within the four obedient shires, namely, Dublin, Louth, Meath, and Kildare, which formed the Pale, were regarded as subjects entitled to the protection of English law; all others were styled and regarded as "Irish enemies." In the process of time, however, by special grants, some of the native septs were permitted to have the benefit of English laws—the O'Neals of Ulster, O'MacLouglin of Munster, O'Conors of Connaught, O'Briens of Thomond, and MacMorroughs of Leinster.

In the reign of King John, it seems a writ ordered that the benefits of English law should be conferred on the Irish generally. A chancellor was appointed in the third year of the reign of Henry III., A.D. 1219. He was the highest legal

[1] *Lives of the Lord Chancellors of Ireland.*

functionary of the realm, Keeper of the Great Seal, and Speaker of the House of Lords.

The Court of Justice sat first in the Castle of Dublin, which included the palace of the viceroy, a fortress for the defence of the city, the Courts of Justice for the adjudication of suits and the trials of offenders, and a chapel with two chaplains, a hall for the Privy Council and Parliaments; but the early Parliaments had no fixed place of assembling. They sometimes sat in Christ Church, Dublin, at the city of Kilkenny, or at Drogheda. They were held by commission from the King of England, who certified to the viceroy the occasion on which he desired the attendance of members. The summons was by writs directed to the sheriffs of counties, issued by the viceroy and council, requiring those summoned to treat of things proposed by them. The Irish Parliament consisted of the king, represented by his viceroy, the Lords Spiritual and Temporal, the former including abbots and priors. The members of the House of Commons were knights of shires, citizens, and burgesses. Abbots, priors, and proctors sat in the fifteenth century, the latter not taking part in the debates, but rendering advice if called on.

Absentees, who did not obey the summons to attend Parliament, were fined. In the ninth year of the reign of Edward III., the Bishop of Emly was fined for non-attendance. On the Memorandum Roll it is set forth that on the Vigil of the Nativity, as the bishop was riding to the church, his palfrey stumbled and threw him to the earth, whereby he was grievously wounded, and three of his ribs were broken; in consequence, during the whole session, he lay so sick that his life was despaired of, and without peril of his body he could not approach the Parliament. His petition was favourably considered by the king, who, in consideration of the bishop's injury, ordered the fine to be remitted.

During the reign of Henry III. (1219) considerable benefits were conferred on the colonists, as well also on the natives of Ireland. Magna Charta, the great charter granted by John at the command of the lords of England, was granted to Ireland, and also the benefit of the laws of England to the natives of Ireland.

CHAPTER II.

1275–1478.

Wogan's Parliament—The Statute of Kilkenny—The Viceroyalty of the Duke of York—His Popularity—Birth of the Duke of Clarence in 1449—His Baptism—Claim of Independent Legislation—The Earl of Desmond.—His Intimacy with Edward IV.—Rash Answer to the King—The Queen's Resolve—Earl of Worcester Viceroy—Earl of Desmond tried and executed—"The Butcher of England"—His Fate—Eulogy of Caxton.

THE Parliament of 1295, called by Sir John Wogan, then viceroy, may be regarded as the first regular Parliament held in Ireland. Though, as we learn from the historical review of the Irish legislative system, by the Right Hon. Mr. Ball, the representative constitution of this Parliament was continued, as time went on writs were not always issued to the same counties and towns. As might have been expected, the native Irish were not representatives in these early Parliaments. These Parliaments appear to have their inception from the king addressed to the Privy Council, as to what laws were required to be enacted. This Parliament met at Kilkenny, when the notices enacted the celebrated statute called by that name. It declares that many of the English of Ireland, discarding the English tongue, manners, style of riding, laws, and usages, lived and governed themselves according to the mode, fashion, and language of the Irish enemies, and also made divers marriages and alliances with them, whereby the lands and the liege people thereof, the English language, the allegiance due to their lord the King of England, and the English laws then were put in subjection and decayed, and the Irish enemies exalted, and raised up contrary to reason. The statute then prohibited alliance by marriage, gossipred,[1] fostering of children between English and Irish, under penalty of treason; also selling to the Irish horses, armour, or victuals, under a like penalty. All Englishmen or Irish living among them were to use the English language, be called by English names, follow the English customs, and use saddles in riding. If ecclesiastics dwelling among the English did not use the English language, the profits of their benefices were to be seized by their superiors, but they had respite to learn the English language.

The effect of this statute was to banish the language, usages and sports, the music and festive meetings between the Irish and English.

In 1449 Richard, Duke of York, was appointed viceroy. He was accompanied by the duchess and his children, and he soon showed a desire to treat the Irish with kindness. This had the natural

[1] Standing godfather or godmother for children.

effect. The heart of man leaps kindly back to kindness, and the Irish chiefs entered into friendly relations with the princely viceroy. Maginnis of Iveagh, MacMahon of Farney, MacArtan, O'Reilly, O'Flanagan of Turah, and other Irish chiefs were glad to treat with him on friendly terms. The O'Byrnes of Wicklow engaged to have the laws of England observed in their territory, and the chief promised his wife should wear the English dress and learn the English language. The viceroy was so popular it was declared that in twelve months the wildest Irishman would be sworn an Englishman; and when the duke's son, George of York, Duke of Clarence, was born in Dublin Castle, on 12th October 1449, aware of the Irish regard for the affinity of gossipred, despite the statute of Kilkenny, he procured the chief of the great rival houses—the Earls of Desmond and Ormond, FitzGerald and Butler, the Irish Guelphs and Ghibelline —to be sponsors of the infant prince.

We learn from Mr. Gilbert's able work, *The Viceroys of Ireland*, that, stimulated by the presence and position of the duke, the Parliament publicly enunciated the independence of the legislature in Ireland, and asserted rights which had hitherto been suffered to lie in abeyance, owing to the relations of the colonists with England. Having asserted the right to their own coinage in Ireland, distinct from that of England, the Parliament formally declared that, as Normandy and Guienne when under the obedience of England were separate from its laws and statutes, so also in Ireland, though under the obedience of the same realm, was nevertheless separate from its laws and statutes, except such as were, by the Lords Spiritual and Temporal, and Commons of Ireland, freely admitted and accepted in their Parliaments and great councils.

The Parliament further declared that, according to ancient prescription, the king's subjects in Ireland were not bound to answer writs, except those under the Great Seal of Ireland; and that any officer attempting to put decrees from England into force in Ireland should incur forfeiture of all his Irish property, and be fined one thousand marks. Appeals of treason were confined to the constable and marshal of Ireland, and while the Duke of York resided as viceroy in Ireland,[1] he was to be respected as king. When the alternate fortunes of the Wars of the Roses brought the house of York again in the ascendant, Edward, son of the popular viceroy, was King Edward IV.

The Earl of Desmond was no exception to the high character of the other members of this distinguished family. He was brave in the fight, and wise in the senate. He had fought in many a well-contested field, and at tilt and tourney was distinguished for his knightly accomplishments. During a visit to England, while staying in London he felt it his duty to pay his respects to the sovereign.

He was related by marriage to King Edward IV., by whom he was much beloved for his gallantry in

[1] *Lives of the Lord Chancellors*, vol. i. p. 108.

the field and wisdom in the council. This king was of an amorous disposition, and fell in love with the beautiful Elizabeth Woodville, widow of Sir John Grey of Groby. Finding the lady too pure to yield to his illicit proposals, King Edward IV. married her, and, finding the alliance was not regarded as worthy of his position as England's king, and that his subjects looked coldly on the lovely queen, the king asked his friend Desmond's advice on the matter.

Desmond strongly advised the king to strengthen his position by alliance with a foreign princess, and hinted at a divorce from his newly-made queen. The king, however, as a Catholic, remained true to his marriage vows, and the Earl of Desmond was destined to suffer for his worldly advice. On some provocation from the queen, the king unguardedly said—

"Your pride, madam, would be humbled had I followed the advice of my cousin of Desmond."

"What advice was that, prithee?" quoth the queen.

"Nay, that must not be told," said the king. But, alas! the words sank deep into the mind of the queen, and when, later on, she moulded the king to her humour, she gradually found out the secret advice of the unfortunate Desmond. It rankled in her breast, and aroused an inordinate desire for vengeance. The graces of Desmond's person—he was one of the handsomest men of his time, and the gifts of his mind, for he was very accomplished

—availed nothing to allay her thirst for vengeance. The opportunity soon presented itself.

John Tiptoft, Earl of Worcester, a man of illustrious birth and large fortune, possessed a cruel and relentless heart. The queen was not slow to impress upon him ideas of hostility towards Desmond. Worcester, too, was related to the king, and the crafty queen represented him as sure of Edward's chief favour if Desmond was out of the way. To further her intentions, she procured the removal of Desmond from the office of viceroy in Ireland, and caused the Earl of Worcester to be appointed in his stead. This gave him the requisite power to accomplish her aim against Desmond. The new chief governor caused a Parliament to be assembled at Drogheda, one of the chief towns of the Pale, remote from the south of Ireland, the territory where the Earl of Desmond's power lay. This servile Parliament, under the viceroy's control, speedily entertained articles of impeachment of treason against the earl for violation of the statute of Kilkenny, by fosterages and alliances with the king's Irish enemies. The earl was at once attainted as a traitor, and condemned to death. He was quickly beheaded by the commands of Worcester at Drogheda, on the 14th February 1467.

Retribution was promptly at hand. The treasurer of Ireland, FitzEustace, Lord Portlester, was allied to the Geraldines by the marriage of his daughter with the Earl of Kildare, and he was accused before

Worcester with having incited the late Earl of Desmond to assume the title of King of Ireland. This charge was boldly denied by the treasurer, and fell to the ground. The Earl of Worcester was recalled into England, and employed in trying a number of the adherents of the house of Lancaster. He did so with such barbarity that he obtained the *soubriquet* of " The Butcher of England."

When Henry VI. once more occupied the throne in 1470, "the Butcher" sought to conceal himself. His character was so odious, both in England and Ireland, that he knew there was no chance of his life being spared if he was discovered. He avoided the city, he shunned the town, he sought shelter in the forest, and supported life as best he could. Even these precautions did not tend to prolong his miserable existence. He was discovered crouching, like some bird of night, among the branches of a lofty tree in the forest of Havering. With shouts of execration he was hurried to London, and stowed away in one of the deepest dungeons in the Tower.

Impatient to rid the earth of "the Butcher," Worcester was speedily brought to trial. How strange are the revolutions of Fortune's wheel! In the chamber wherein he was tried for his life he presided, only four years previously, at the trial of De Vere, Earl of Oxford. The earl was then found guilty, and by him condemned to death; and lo! the son and successor of this earl was presiding as judge now. Well might he exclaim, *Tempora mutantur!* His trial was short—his sentence sure; he was beheaded on Tower Hill.

So few were able to say a good word for "the Butcher," that I cannot forbear extracting the account William Caxton, the printer, gives of how the earl passed his last hours on earth. Had we not known so much of his antecedents, we might imagine the worthy printer referred to some totally different peer, for he describes the Earl of Worcester as one who "flowered in virtue, so that none was like unto him among the lords of the temporality in science and moral virtue. What great loss was it of that noble and virtuous and well-disposed lord, and what worship had he in Rome, in the presence of our Holy Father the Pope, and so in all places unto his death, every man there might learn to die and take his death patiently, wherein I hope and doubt not but that God received his soul into His everlasting bliss, for, as I am informed, he right advisedly ordained all his things, as well for his last will of worldly goods as to his soul's health, and patiently and holily without grudging in charity, before that he departed out of this world. I beseech Almighty God to have mercy on his soul, and pray all them that shall hear or read this little treatise, much virtuous of friendship, in likewise of your charity to remember his soul among your prayers."[1]

I am afraid few adherents of the house of Desmond would respond "Amen" to that prayer. They believed the terrible fate of "the Butcher"

[1] *Tullius His Book of Friendship*, printed by Caxton, 1481.

was the just judgment of Heaven upon the cruel murderer of the beloved Earl of Desmond. The Irish Parliament also sought to atone for the injustice, by enacting that all the possessions of the Earl of Worcester in Ireland should be given to the Earl of Kildare, in compensation for the injustice he sustained at the hands of the earl; and Lambay Island, which had been given to him, was restored to the Archbishop of Dublin.

CHAPTER III.

1478–1534.

State of the Anglo-Norman Colony, A.D. 1478—Rival Viceroys summon Parliament—Anecdote of Dean Cobbe—State of Religion in 1484—Lambert Simnel crowned King, 1487—Perils of Members of Parliament—Henry VII.—Viceroy Sir Edward Poynings—Mode of proceeding in Parliament—A Bridle on the Irish Parliament—Royal Favours on Sir Edward Poynings.

WE can hardly imagine greater anarchy than prevailed in the colony at this time. Lord Grey, as lord-deputy, landed in Ireland in 1478, with a guard of three hundred archers and men-at-arms. He did well to have them, for the Irish Privy Council selected the Earl of Kildare as viceroy, and refused to acknowledge Lord Grey. The chancellor, Lord Portlester, who was father-in-law of the Earl of Kildare, refused to surrender the Great Seal of Ireland, and James Keating, the constable of Dublin Castle, would not allow Lord Grey to enter it. He broke down the drawbridge, and defied the lord-deputy and his guard to enter. For a time both viceroys tried to execute the Irish Government. The Earl of Kildare took a bold step. He summoned a Parliament, which assembled at Naas, in the county of Kildare, in June 1478, which voted him a subsidy. Lord Grey was not idle. He procured the king's writ, commanding Kildare not to act as deputy. The mayor of Dublin was ordered to make public proclamation that no subsidy was to be paid to the Earl of Kildare. Lord Grey summoned a Parliament, which met at Trim, in the county of Meath, where the proceedings of the Naas Parliament were declared null and void. The statutes and ordinances of the Parliament at Naas were ordered by the judges to be cancelled, and delivered up on pain of felony. A new Great Seal was engraved by Thomas Archbold, master of the mint, which the Parliament ordered to be the Great Seal of Ireland.

A prebendary named Cobbe removed the cross from Christ's Church Cathedral, Dublin, and supplied its place with a boar's head and a crown, which occasioned the following epigram :—

"Christ's cross from Christ's Church cursed Cobbe hath pulled down,
And placed in its stead what he worships—the crown.
Avenging the cause of the Gadarine people,
This miscreant hath placed a swine's head on the steeple ;
By this intimating to all who pass by,
That his hearers are swine,—and his church is a sty." [1]

We may judge from that conduct on the part of the Dean of Christ's Church what was the state of

[1] Gilbert's *History of Dublin*, vol. i. p. 285.

religion in Ireland. This also is disclosed by an Act passed in 1484, reciting that "divers benefices and advowsons of the Sees were situated amongst Irish enemies, and as no Englishman could inhabit the said benefices, and divers English clerks, who were enabled to have cure of souls, were not expert in the Irish language, and such of them as were, disdained to inhabit amongst the Irish people, and others dared not."

About this time, a youth of fair presence and gentle bearing, who was presented to the head of the Geraldines, the Earl of Kildare, then Viceroy of Ireland, as the Earl of Warwick, and gave such strong proofs of his being so, was treated as such. Not only did the Earl of Kildare espouse his cause, but the viceroy's brother, Sir Thomas FitzGerald of Laccagh, Lord Chancellor of Ireland, also believed him to be the true heir of the house of York. Numerous men of rank, influenced by these dignitaries, pledged themselves to aid him with their lives and fortunes. They also applied to Margaret, Dowager Duchess of Burgundy, sister of the Duke of Clarence and aunt to the young Earl of Warwick. This princess acknowledged the youth as her nephew, and supplied a force of two thousand men under the command of Martin Swartz, a general of rank and military skill.

The Earl of Lincoln, Lord Lovel, and other adherents of the White Rose, embarked with the army of Swartz, and landed in Dublin in May 1487. The coronation of the young king took place with royal splendour in Christ's Church Cathedral on Whit-Sunday, May 24, 1487. He received the title of Edward VI. The deputy, chief officers of state, judges, and other high functionaries renounced their allegiance to Henry VII., and did homage to the crowned king. A sermon suitable to the event was preached by the Bishop of Meath.

War against the usurper was soon declared. The chancellor changed the mace for the sword, and became a general commanding a division of the Irish troops. These, with the Burgundians under Swartz, landed in Lancashire, and once more the adherents of the rival Roses were to meet in the shock of war. They encountered each other near Stoke, a village about a mile from Newark-on-Trent, and it was a desperate conflict. For three hours the issue seemed doubtful, but the house of Lancaster prevailed. The young aspirant to royalty was taken prisoner; the valiant ex-chancellor was slain, as was also the greater number of the supporters of the claimant, who was discovered to be the child of Thomas Simnel, an Oxford joiner. His fate is involved in obscurity—some stated he was made a turnspit in the royal kitchen, others that he was kept a prisoner in the Tower; but this was his last appearance as a claimant to the throne.

The position of members who had any distance to travel to the Irish Parliament in the reign of Henry VII. was by no means safe or agreeable.

In 1480, the state of the colony was deplorable. The chancellor was at variance with the chief justice of the King's Bench, and the Irish displayed such hostility to the settlers of the Pale, that the cities and boroughs sought to be allowed to refrain from sending members to Parliament, on the ground that their representatives could not encounter the great peril incurred from the king's Irish enemies and English rebels; for it is openly known how great and frequent mischief have been done on the way, both in the north, south, east, and west parts, by reason whereof they may not send proctors, knights, or burgesses.

Prior to the reign of Henry VII., the government of Ireland was confined to the chiefs of Anglo-Norman descent, who exercised almost royal rule. These were the FitzGeralds, Earls of Kildare and Desmond; the Butlers, Earls of Ormond; De Burgh, Earl of Clanrickarde; De Lacys, St. Lawrence, and others, who sometimes yielded obedience, or sometimes thwarted the action of the viceroy. When Henry VII. was firmly established, he learned, with more minuteness than his predecessors, the state of Ireland. He found the Privy Council, composed of men of the highest rank in Church and State, having no check imposed by the presence of the sovereign, often overruled the deputy and controlled the Parliament.

To be a privy councillor it was desired; to be a member of Parliament was shunned. Henry VII. resolved to alter this; to make the Irish people more free, and less dependent on the lords. He also had complaints made of the great expense incurred by the viceroys assuming to themselves the power of convening Parliaments, and imposing subsidies for non-attendance, and of the great expense incurred by members having to attend frequently in Dublin or elsewhere. He therefore selected a deputy, Sir Edward Poynings, to reform these grievances. He arrived in Ireland in 1494, and called a Parliament, which met at Drogheda, and passed the celebrated statute 10 Henry VII., called Poynings' Law. By this all statutes made within the realm of England concerning the common weal, from henceforth be deemed good and effectual in the law, and such be accepted, used, and executed within the land of Ireland in all points, according to the tenor of the same. By this Act all the fundamental laws of England were transferred to bind Ireland. This is eulogised by Lord Coke as a profitable Act of Parliament. He further provided that no Parliament be holden in the said land, but at such season as the king's lieutenant and council there first do certify the king under the Great Seal of that land, the causes and consideration and all such acts as seemeth should pass in the said Parliament, and such causes, considerations, and acts affirmed by the king and his council to be good and expedient for that land; and to summon the said Parliament under his Great Seal; that done, a Parliament to be had and holden after the form afore rehearsed, and if any Parliament be held contrary, it is to be deemed void and of none effect. The effect of this, according to the opinion of the late Lord Chief Justice Whiteside, was to place a bridle in the mouth of the Irish Parliament, and subjugate alike the lord-deputy, the nobles, and the commoners to the will of the king's council at London.

Sir Edward Poynings received many tokens of the king's favour. He was a privy councillor, a knight of the Garter, and, with the Archbishop of Canterbury, Warham, ambassador to the Emperor Maximilian. He went to Ireland as deputy for the king's son, afterwards Henry VIII.

CHAPTER IV.

1534–1537.

Henry VIII. Head of the Church—Dr. Brown, Archbishop of Dublin—Irish refuse to renounce the Pope—The Archbishop's Letter to Cromwell—Lord Leonard Grey, Viceroy — Catholic Ceremonies observed — Parliament in 1537 — Henry VIII. made King of Ireland — Statute respecting Absentee Proprietors—Effect of that Statute.

HENRY VIII., having taken the title of Head of the Church, in A.D. 1534 appointed Dr. Brown, who had been an Augustinian friar, but was changed by Henry's conclusive mode of conduct into a zealous Protestant, Archbishop of Dublin. He was specially commissioned that it was the royal will and pleasure that his Majesty's subjects in Ireland, and even those in England, should obey his commands in spiritual as in temporal matters, and renounce their allegiance to the Pope of Rome. The failure of this mandate may be judged from the archbishop's letter to Lord Cromwell. He wrote on December 1535, "that he had endeavoured, almost at the risk of his temporal life, to procure the nobility and gentry of this nation to due obedience, to obey his Highness as Supreme Head, as well spiritual as temporal, but I could prevail nothing as yet."

The Irish Parliament, summoned by Henry's viceroy, Lord Leonard Grey, met in 1537, and adopted all the commands of Henry VIII. He was made by statute Supreme Head of the Church, entitled to the first fruits of bishoprics and other revenues of the Church in Ireland. The revenues of suppressed religious houses were vested in the Crown, and his title from this point, hitherto lord of Ireland, was changed to that of king. In the Parliament summoned in 1541, Sir Thomas Cusack, who had filled the chair as Speaker in Lord Grey's Parliament, was again elected. Great ceremonies were used when opening the Irish Parliament at this time, which would startle our present House of Commons. The Houses met on Corpus Christi Thursday, a holiday of obligation in the Catholic Church. After morning mass, the lord-deputy was escorted from the church by the lord chancellor, the archbishop, the bishops, the judges, and a numerous retinue of guards. In the procession rode the Earls of Ormond and Desmond, the Lords Barry, Roche, FitzMaurice, and Birmingham, and members of the Privy Council. As there were several Irish members present who were not acquainted with the English language, the Earl of Ormond acted as interpreter, and translated the message from the king, delivered to the lords by Alan, Lord Chancellor, and by the Speaker, Sir

Thomas Cusack, speeches which the Irish members received greatly to their contentation.

The alteration in the royal title having been announced, the Speaker and members of the House of Commons withdrew to their own House, when the lords proceeded to pass the Bill changing the king's title from that of lord to king of Ireland. We learn from the State papers of Henry VIII. that the proctors, bishops, and abbots, who were summoned to meet the Royal Commission in Parliament, May 18th, 1537, so strictly opposed the Act of Supremacy, that a letter from Dublin was addressed to Lord Cromwell, stating the lord-deputy was compelled to prorogue the Parliament. This at once caused an order to be directed, under the Great Seal of England, declaring that spiritual proctors should have no vote in Parliament, which was confirmed by the Irish Statute, 28 Henry VIII. c. 12.

Failing to convert the Irish by Act of Parliament, the lord chancellor, the Archbishop of Dublin, and other Protestant members of the Privy Council, undertook a *Converting Circuit*, of which we have this account in the State papers.[1] "We arrived first at Carlow, where the Lord James Butler kept his Christmas; and there being well entertained, from thence we went to Kilkenny, where we were not less entertained by the Earl of Ormond. There, on New Year's Day, the Archbishop of Dublin preached the word of God, having very good

[1] Vol. iii. p. 108.

audience, and published the king's injunctions, and the king's translation of the Pater Noster, the Ave Maria, the Articles of Faith, and the Ten Commandments, in English—divers papers whereof we delivered to the bishop and other prelates of the diocese, commanding them to do the like in other districts. The Saturday following we repaired to Ross, which town having been heretofore one of the best towns of this land, being also situated in the best place of these parts for subduing the Kavanaghs, is in manners utterly decayed and waste, by reason of the continual war and annoyance of the Kavanaghs, which cannot be helped while the Kavanaghs remain unreformed. Then the morning after, the said archbishop preached; that night we went to Wexford, where the archbishop preached and delivered the injunctions; and on to Waterford, where they were well entertained, the mayor and his brethren having great obedience. On Sunday, the archbishop again preached, and published the king's injunctions. Next day we kept the sessions both for the city and the shire, where was put to execution four *felons*, accompanied with *another*, a friar, whom, among the residue, we commanded to be hanged in his habit, and so to remain upon the gallows for a mirror to all his brethren to live truly."[1]

It cannot cause surprise this mode of instructing the benighted papists to confession to the creed of Henry VIII., hanging monks as felons, and having

[1] *Lives of the Lord Chancellors of Ireland*, vol. i. p. 191.

them hanged in their habits, *pour encourager les autres*, did not cause many conversions.

The Parliament, during the reign of Henry VIII., passed a stringent law against absentees. Receiving rents through agents was regarded criminal, and English noblemen, who, by marriage or descent, acquired lands in Ireland, on which they never resided, were required to assign them to persons resident in Ireland. The statute declared that if such was not done, the lands of all such as disobeyed were forfeited.[1]

The case of the estates of absentees was brought before the English judges in a case reported in the 12th Part of Lord Coke's Reports. The case was that of the Earl of Shrewsbury and Waterford, when, "It was resolved by the judges of England, to whom the question was by the Privy Council referred, that the Irish Act against absentees did not only take away from the Earl of Waterford the possessions which were given to him at the time of his creation, but also the dignity itself." The Court said, "It was with good reason to take away such dignity by Act of Parliament; and although the said Earl of Shrewsbury be not only of great honour and virtue, but also of great possessions in England, yet it was not the intention of the Act to continue him earl in Ireland when his possessions were taken from him."

[1] 28 Henry VIII. c. 77.

CHAPTER V.

1537–1603.

Reigns of Edward VI., Queen Mary, and Queen Elizabeth—Mary's Efforts to restore the Catholic Religion—The Queen requests the Pope to send a Bull restoring England to the Catholic Faith—Parliament repeals the Statute declaring Henry VIII. Head of the Church—Cardinal Pole invested with the Pallium—Archbishop Vaughan also—Anecdote of Dean Cole, and how his Mission was thwarted—Accession of Queen Elizabeth—Forfeited Estates of the Earl of Desmond—Royal Grants to Raleigh and Spenser—Kilcolman Castle—Costume in House of Lords and Commons—Planting the forfeited Estates—Angry Letter from the Queen to the Archbishop of Dublin—Perrot's Parliament in 1586—Members of House of Common—Irish Chiefs attend—Attempt to evade Poynings' Law—Viceroy applies for Archbishop's Recall — Tried for High Treason — Found Guilty — Sentenced—The Queen's Clemency.

I DO not find mention of any Irish Parliament during the short reign of Edward VI. It is worthy of note that, although the Catholics regained full power and the practice of their religion, on the crown of England descending to Henry's daughter by his first wife, Catherine of Aragon, no instance of intolerance can be traced in Ireland, though the evil spirit of persecution was rife in England. As was quite a matter of course, and to be expected, after the accession of Mary to the throne, on the death of King Edward VI., a Parliament met in Dublin on June 1, 1557, and repealed all the statutes passed since the 20th year of King Henry VIII. against the Pope and the Catholic religion. The statute declared that the title of Supreme Head of the Church was not justly attributable to any king or civil governor. An Act was passed which regulated ecclesiastic matters, with a proviso which displays most singular moderation—" That this Act should not extend to, or affect in any way, such grants of ecclesiastical property as had been made by the Crown to private individuals, or to any public or civil corporation."

It may be some guarantee to those in our day who dread any display of Catholic ascendancy when Ireland gains Home Rule, to recollect that, though in Queen Mary's reign the Catholic faith in Ireland was fully established, yet no single case of persecution against those who remained steadfast in the Protestant faith occurred.

At the request of Queen Mary, the then Pope Paul VI. sent a papal Bull restoring the queen's dominions to the ancient faith, and submission to the See of Rome. The bearer of this treasure was Cardinal Pole, an Englishman of noble birth, who had lately received the Pallium, a dignity not conferred since on any Englishman for two centuries and a half, but is now worthily borne by another

Englishman of noble birth, His Eminence Cardinal Vaughan, Archbishop of Westminister.

Though Romanism was stained by bigotry in England, no intolerance was shown Protestant doctrine in Ireland. Nay, such was the toleration of the Irish, that many English families, friends of the Reformation, fled to Ireland for, and found protection among, the Irish Catholics. Leland in his History relates an amusing story, that the Dean of St. Paul's, Cole, was directed to go to Ireland, armed with a commission to persecute heretics. While halting at Chester on his way to Dublin, he showed his commission at the inn he occupied, in the presence of the landlady. She had Protestant relatives, who, like many others, sought refuge in Ireland, and naturally feared for their safety. Resolved to frustrate the design, she contrived to abstract the commission from the dean's box, and placed in its stead a pack of cards. The dean, when before the Irish Privy Council, stated the instructions he received when leaving London, and produced the box which had held the royal commission, and empowering the Privy Council to enforce the authority of the queen, and lo! when opened, the pack of cards fell fluttering on the table. The irreverent burst of laughter added to the dean's chagrin. We may guess his confusion and the surprise of the council, who felt relieved by the trick evidently practised on the dean. The death of the queen put an end to any attempt to renew the commission.

Queen Mary died in 1558, after an unhappy reign. The loss of Calais seems to have greatly affected her. She said the name was written on her heart.

On the accession of Queen Elizabeth in A.D. 1558, the condition of affairs in Ireland were not favourable to English rule. Revolt took place in Munster, where the Earl of Desmond had a powerful army, and some of Elizabeth's forces were defeated. The Earl of Essex, the viceroy, was recalled, and it is said the queen so forgot her position as a queen, and her decorum as a lady, as to give him a slap on the ears, which caused him to exclaim, "I would not suffer such conduct from your father." As was expected, the English throne being occupied by a Protestant queen, all that had been done to restore the ancient faith to the churches in Ireland was now changed. The statues, pictures, and other marks of Catholic piety were removed from the Cathedral of St. Patrick's and Christ's Church, in Dublin, and the officials, with due alacrity, from being zealous Catholics of Queen Mary, were speedily converted into equally sturdy Protestants under Queen Elizabeth. The forfeiture incurred by the revolt of the Earl of Desmond placed over four hundred thousand acres of land at the disposal of the Government, and the queen was able to bestow eleven thousand acres on Sir Walter Raleigh, who had served her Majesty in Ireland. This large grant included the towns of Lismore and Youghal, where Sir Walter built a residence on the plan of his birthplace in Devonshire, now the property of the family of the late Sir John Pope Hennessey, M.P. The poet Edmund Spenser, author of the *Faery Queen*, who had not been well treated by the close-fisted treasurer, had also a grant of four thousand acres in County Cork. It is said, when he wrote his poem he sent it to the queen, with a request he should have some remuneration for his work. The queen directed Lord Burleigh "to give him a reasonable sum." Finding this not complied with, Spenser sought to get back his poem. This, too, was unnoticed; so the poet addressed the queen in these lines:—

> "I was promised on a time,
> Some reason for my rhyme;
> From that time to this season,
> I neither had rhyme nor reason."

The forfeiture of the Desmond estates made Spenser proprietor of the Castle of Kilcolman, near Buttevant, in the county of Cork. His antipathy towards his Irish neighbours, as disclosed in his writings, induced them to burn his castle, and he and his family, with the exception of one child, fled into England, where he died. He is buried in Westminster Abbey. The Hydes and Bechers, now owners of Castle Hyde, also had valuable grants from the Desmond estates.

It does not appear that at this period there was any fixed place of meeting, as we find the Parliaments summoned to meet, now in Dublin, now in Drogheda,

Trim, Naas, or Kilkenny. It is reserved for our
day to have members endeavouring to obtain a seat
within the House of Commons of Westminster,
which does not suffice to hold the members at
present entitled to represent them in the faithful
Commons, so no doubt they will be relieved from
the plethora by the removal of greater numbers of
the Irish members. Some discussion has lately
been excited by the attempt to secure a seat by the
deposit of a hat, a card, or a book. The attention
of the Speaker has been called, and it is said he
considers the hat should be the walking hat usually
worn by the member, not a duplicate used for the
purpose of securing the seat. It was not merely
as regarded the order of legislation that Poynings'
Parliament took action. It was discovered that
for many years the peers of Parliament, Spiritual
and Temporal, had ceased to appear in their robes,
to the great dishonour of the House of Lords.
They were therefore compelled to wear their
respective robes; and I presume some such enactment,
either express or implied, was presented for the
members of the House of Commons. In this respect
we are able to state that up to the time of the Union,
the Irish members attended in court dress. Those
members who had Orders displayed the stars and
ribbons, wore them both in the Lords and Commons, and the members wore their swords. Rather
singular that in what was long regarded as the
first assembly of gentlemen in the world, all should
wear their hats except the Speaker, who wears a

courtly robe and a long wig. We learn from Sir Nathanael Wrexall, he felt deeply shocked when he beheld the House in 1780, with the knights, citizens, and burgesses clad in great-coats, frocks, and wearing boots. We have a tradition of the member for New Ross in Ireland, who, during a violent contest between the Irish Government and the Nationalist members in the time of Lord Chesterfield, in 1757, after riding post from his residence to Dublin, and not having time to change his attire before the division was taken, strode into the House as he was attired, recorded his vote, which thereby the National party defeated the Government, giving the Nationalists the narrow majority of one. He is yet remembered in popular memory as "Tottenham in his boots."

As the Irish never neglect an opportunity of giving expression to their loyalty to the throne, they readily availed themselves of the royal trust. Public and private rejoicings took place in Dublin. Bonfires blazed, feasts were given, cannon and musketry were loud, bells rang merry peals, and theatricals such as were likely to amuse the populace took place. The pageant entitled "The Nine Worthies" shows a curious jumble of sacred and profane notabilities, namely, Hector, Alexander the Great, Julius Cæsar, Joshua, David, Judas Maccabæus, King Arthur, Charlemagne, and Godfrey of Bouillon. There was tilting for the knights, and all display denoted loyalty to the king.

Not that the king, at his pleasure, might confer

as well the dignity as the possessions to any other for the defence of the said realm. On this question the late Chief Justice Whiteside, in his Lecture on the Irish Parliament,[1] says: "The propriety of this decision came before the House of Lords at Westminster in 1832, in the case of the Earl of Shrewsbury, claiming as Earl of Waterford, to vote at the election of representative peers of Ireland, and it was held that the dignity of the peerage was not taken away by the Irish Act against absentees; and that the opinion above cited was not binding in the House of Lords, or any other court of justice, which was read in English and in Irish. It was unanimously agreed to, and, being read three times in the Lords, was committed to the Commons, who were equally willing to pass it. Next day it was read in *plain*[2] Parliament, before the Lords and Commons, before it received the assent of the lord-deputy."

Shortly after Elizabeth's accession to the throne, a Parliament was assembled in Dublin, at which the statutes enacted during the reign of Queen Mary for the restoration of the Catholic religion were repealed, and the queen's supremacy as "Head of the Church" was established. We learn from Mr. Jenning's very able and entertaining work, *Anecdotes of the British Parliament*, the prompt action of Henry VIII. to cause the dilatory members of the House of Commons to pass an Act for the

---

[1] *Life and Death of the Irish Parliament*, part i. p. 41.
[2] Probably for plein (full).

suppression of monasteries. So I am able to give a proof that Henry's daughter, Queen Elizabeth, was also able to bring an Irish archbishop to obey her commands. Finding Dr. Loftus, whom she appointed Archbishop of Dublin, delaying to comply with her request that he should resign the deanery of St. Patrick's in favour of Dr. Weston, whom she selected as Lord Chancellor of Ireland, she wrote to the archbishop the following brief but very emphatic letter:—

"REVEREND PRELATE,—I understand you are backward in complying with your agreement; but I would have you to know that I, who have made you what you are, can unmake you, and if you do not forthwith fulfil your engagement, by —— I will unfrock you.—Yours, if you demean yourself,

"ELIZABETH."[1]

This letter had the desired effect, and Dr. Weston was speedily Dean of St. Patrick's.

Queen Elizabeth adopted the plan, subsequently carried out by her successor James I., of obliging the grantees of the Irish forfeited estates to plant them with English or Scotch colonists. She also prohibited the daughters of such colonists from intermarrying with Irishmen for two descents.

In the Parliament which met in Dublin A.D. 1585, known as Perrot's Parliament, we find the most perfect account of the members of Lords and Commons. As after the suppression of monasteries by Henry

[1] *London Society*, vol. ix. p. 500.

VIII. no abbot was summoned, the Lords consisted of bishops and temporal peers. At this Parliament in the Lords were twenty-six bishops, and the same number of temporal peers. Of these were four Irish lords. Owing to the great number of counties formed in Ireland during the reigns of Mary and Elizabeth, there sat in the House of Commons no less than fifty-four members for twenty-seven counties, and seventy-two from thirty-six cities and boroughs, making a total of a hundred and twenty-six. The names of several members denote Irish members.[1] Possibly the presence of the Irish chiefs in Perrot's Parliament induced the spirit of resistance to the lord-deputy, which did not take place with his predecessors. Poynings' Law was not inflexible; it had been occasionally dispensed with, and Sir John Perrot sought to do so with his Parliament. He wanted to get some Acts passed, but the House was not complaisant, and he could not bring any members to obedience. This did not please the queen, and I have given a specimen of her epistolary style when her will was thwarted. It is likely she addressed the viceroy in such words, as unfortunately when drinking at the council table he was heard to say of the queen, " She may command what she list, but we will do as we like." At another time he said, " This fiddling woman troubles me out of measure; it is not safe for her Majesty to break such hard bread to her servants."

[1] *Historical Review* by Ball, pp. 15, 16, and note in Appendix, p. 265.

He was also charged with designing to suppress St. Patrick's Cathedral. Finding himself greatly disconcerted by the chancellor, Archbishop Loftus, he besought the queen to recall him; and on his visiting London a charge of high treason for seeking to weaken the queen's authority in Ireland, was preferred against him. A prosecution, conducted by Sir John Puckering, queen's serjeant, was brought on the strength of those rash expressions. Aware of the weak case against the accused, the queen's serjeant tried to influence the jury with the words used. "For," he said, "the original of his treasons proceeded from the imagination of his heart, which imagination was in itself high treason, without the prisoner proceeding to overt act; and the heart being possessed with his traitorous imagination, and not being able to contain itself, burst forth in vile and traitorous speeches, for *ex abundantia cordis os loquitur.*"

In reference to the charge of designing to suppress the Cathedral of St. Patrick's, Perrot said the archbishop, who was his mortal foe, derived a revenue of eight hundred marks a year from it; and he, the viceroy, wished to make it the site of the proposed University of Dublin, now Trinity College. The jury having retired, in less than an hour brought in the verdict finding the prisoner guilty! The dread sentence was pronounced but not executed. The queen, on reading the report of the trial, remembered the rescript of the Emperor Theodosius, which, she said, should rule this case: "If any person speak ill of the emperor through a foolish rashness or inadvertency, it is to be despised; if out of madness, it deserves pity; if from malice, it calls for mercy."[1] It is not often the queen showed such clemency. Some believed Sir John Perrot was a son of Henry VIII.

[1] *Lives of the Lord Chancellors of Ireland*, vol. i. p. 271.

CHAPTER VI.

1603–1644.

Bolton's Statutes—Heads of Bills—Accession of James I.—Disappointed Hopes—Confiscation of Ulster—Parliament in 1613—Contest for the Speakership—Charles I. sends Earl of Strafford as Viceroy—A Parliament in 1639—Serjeant Eustace, Speaker—Strafford encouraging the Linen Industry—Pym threatens—The Commission for Defective Titles—The Galway Jury—High Sheriff dies in Prison—Lord Chancellor and others impeached—Articles of Impeachment—Their Failure—Strafford and Charles I. executed.

THE valuable treatise, attributed to Lord Chancellor Bolton, but believed to be the production of a very eminent Catholic barrister, named Patrick Darcy, appeared in 1644. This treatise underwent consideration from the Irish Lords and Commons. It set forth the laws of England. At this time arose the practice of sending Bills required for Ireland, which, after due consideration by the Irish Privy Council, were submitted for examination by the English Privy Council, who usually sent them to the Attorney-General of England, and, after approval, were returned to the lord-deputy, who sent them to be passed in the Irish Parliament.

Here they had, of course, to be read three times before receiving the royal assent. This roundabout course resulted from Poynings' Law of Henry VII. This was wisely altered, and henceforward only heads of Bills were sent from Parliaments in Ireland under the Stuart kings.

The accession of James I. to the English throne, on the death of Queen Elizabeth, raised the hopes of the Irish Catholics. The son of the hapless Queen of Scots,—whose devoted piety to the Catholic faith made her to be regarded as a martyr; and, in our day, some notion was entertained that she deserved to be canonised,—he was expected, if not to avow himself a Catholic, at least to show respect for its creed. He soon dispelled such notions. While professing himself desirous to give liberty of conscience to his subjects, he declared his hostility to the Mass, the great symbol of Catholic belief, and thus extinguished the hopes of the Catholics of Ireland.

Having resolved on appropriating the province of Ulster, by taking advantage of the alleged treason of the Irish Earls of Tyrone and Tyrconnel, which, even if proved, should not involve the forfeiture of chiefs who were not implicated in this assumed disloyalty, this monarch formed Ulster into nine counties; divided the lands of the native chiefs among his Scotch subjects, who, on his succeeding to the throne of England, naturally expected to profit by his good fortune. But he dared not distribute the estates of the noble English Catholics;

so, having Ulster at his disposal, he turned out the Maguires, O'Hagans, O'Flanagans, O'Neills, MacDonnells, and other Irish chiefs, granting their estates to the Scotch adventurers.

A curious event occurred on the opening of Parliament in May 1613. There were two candidates for the Speakership, Sir John Everard, a popular member, supported by the Catholic party, and Sir John Davis, the Attorney-General, who had all the official Protestant and Government influence. The Nationalists arrived earlier than their opponents, and, availing themselves of this circumstance, proceeded to elect Sir John Everard to the chair. On entering the House, the supporters of the Attorney-General, seeing what had been done, elected their Speaker, being 125 for, to 101 against, his election, and insisted on his sitting in the chair, already occupied by the member previously elected. This, of course, led to very disorderly conduct, but the Attorney-General's party prevailed, and he was regarded as the Speaker.

Having thus colonised Ulster at the expense of the Irish chiefs, he desired the viceroy to state that the king desired to make no distinction between the Anglo-Irish and the English subjects in Ireland. This Parliament revoked the objectionable statute of Kilkenny, and, by statute 13 James I. c. 5, all Acts making any distinction of races between the king's subjects, whether Irish or English born, were annulled. No other Parliament was held in Ireland during the reign of James I.

During the Commonwealth no Parliament was held in Ireland. Cromwell had the country under his iron rule; and during his stay he gave such proofs of his stern will as showed the danger of resistance. By allowing the slaughter of the inhabitants of Drogheda, which lasted for three days, he inspired such terror into the garrisons of other fortified places, they, with one exception, opened their gates at his summons. This exception was Clonmel, which town offered such a gallant resistance, he was about to raise the siege, and retire on Waterford, when, on taking a farewell look at the gallant Tipperary stronghold, he saw something glittering in the grass. On inspection it proved to be a silver button. "Ha!" he said, "if they are using silver buttons, their ammunition must be spent." So it was; having no means of further resistance, the garrison made honourable terms and surrendered.

CHAPTER VII.

1644–1685.

Bolton's Treatise—The Catholic Confederation of Kilkenny in 1642—Cromwell in Ireland—Parliament in Chichester House—Sir Audley Mervyn, Speaker—His Speech—The Adventure Act applied to Ireland—The Confederate Army fight for King Charles I.—Forfeiture of the Estates of the Confederates—The Protestant Bishop of Cork obtains good Terms for the Cromwellians—He receives Thanks of the Lords—Court of Claims—Treasonable Plots.

IMMEDIATELY on the death of King James I., his son Charles I., then a popular and pious prince, succeeded to the throne. By the death of an elder brother, Henry, who was educated by George Buchanan, a very eminent Scotch tutor, Charles became heir; and though it was feared he was too much under the influence of Villiers, Duke of Buckingham, and not of strong intellect, his quiet, gentle disposition made him beloved. He selected as viceroy for Ireland a faithful friend, Sir Thomas Wentworth. In 1639 a Parliament met, and a more orderly election for the Speakership of the Commons took place. Lord Wentworth was viceroy for Charles I.; and the Commons elected Mr. Serjeant Eustace, Speaker, being a wise, learned, and discreet man, of great integrity. On the 26th March, having attended with as many of the members of the House of Commons as wished, he appeared at the bar of the House of Lords. The viceroy sat in state, the peers in their robes, the bishops in lawn. After the usual formalities, the learned Speaker then at great length, with elaborate eloquence, harangued these patient, grave, and reverend seigniors.

Wentworth was soon created Earl of Strafford, and built a large mansion near Naas, in the County Kildare, called at this day the Black Tom's Castle. As he knew he could best serve his royal master, King Charles I., around whose throne the Puritan republicans were hovering, by making grants of land to those likely to support the king, and as Queen Elizabeth had been able to make immense grants in Munster by the forfeiture of the Earl of Desmond's estates, and James I. had driven the natives forth ruthlessly from the fertile province of Ulster, and in these days of arbitrary power of the Crown, Strafford issued a Commission to ascertain defective titles in Connaught, the object being to nullify the titles of the estates throughout Connaught, in order they might be vested in the Crown. The sheriffs of counties were directed to have proper—that is to say, obedient—persons ready for the Commission, and willing to find for the Crown. The plan succeeded in many places; but when the Commission reached Galway, the sheriff had not a jury packed, and those empanelled would not be obedient. The result was the jury were fined heavily. The unfortunate sheriff was both fined and ordered to be confined until he paid the fine, which was so heavy he died in prison. The Irish Parliament was so incensed at the conduct of the lord chancellor, the judges, and the Privy Council, who aided and abetted the inhuman viceroy, they resolved on their impeachment. Another motive also actuated them. The Earl of Strafford was to be tried in England for his conduct, and as it was supposed he would summon many of the Privy Council in Ireland to give evidence on his behalf, the Irish House of Commons prepared articles of impeachment against Sir Richard Bolton, Lord Chancellor; John, Lord Bishop of Derry; Sir Gerard Lowther, Lord Chief Justice of the Common Pleas; and Sir George Ratcliffe, knight. On the 27th February 1640, a committee of forty-four members was appointed by the Commons to prepare the charges, and they lost no time; for on the 4th March they had the following articles drawn up:—

First, that they, the said Sir Richard Bolton, with the others as above named, intending the destruction of the commonwealth of the realm, have traitorously confederated and conspired together to subvert the fundamental laws and government of the kingdom; and, in pursuance thereof, they, and every one of them, have traitorously contrived, introduced, and exercised an arbitrary and tyrannical government against law throughout this kingdom, by the countenance and assistance of Thomas, Earl of Strafford, then chief governor of this kingdom.

Secondly, that they and every of them, the said Sir Richard Bolton, knight, Lord Chancellor of Ireland, and the others, have traitorously assumed to themselves, and every of them, royal power over the goods, persons, lands, and liberties of his Majesty's subjects of this realm; and likewise have maliciously sent a petition to the House requiring that their characters should be cleared from these grave accusations; and after a full debate it was resolved that the House should proceed no further upon the said articles of accusation against the said lord chancellor and chief justice, and thus the formidable impeachment ended.

More important impeachments were carried to a more successful issue. But these events, namely, the impeachment of Strafford and his royal master, do not form the subject of this work. Pym, who had been the intimate friend of Sir Thomas Wentworth while he advocated republican principles, on finding that Wentworth espoused the royal cause, said to him, "So you have left us; I will never leave you while your head remains on your shoulders." The headsman's axe which struck the head off the king and Strafford proved the earnestness of the stern republican promise.

CHAPTER VIII.

1685-1690.

James II. King—Visits Ireland in 1688—Summons a Parliament—The King's Speech—Titles of Statutes—Sir William Petty—Statement respecting Forfeited Estates—William III. King—English Parliament annuls Irish Statutes of King James II.

THE number of Catholic lords and gentlemen who took part in the Confederation of Kilkenny, or who were accused of rebellion in 1641, left a great portion of Ireland for distribution among the Cromwellian party and the London capitalists, who advanced money under the provisions of the Adventure Act.

During the closing years of the reign of Charles I., the forces of the Confederation of Kilkenny, authorised, as they believed, by authority from the king, took up arms in his cause, and, under the military skill of the famous General Owen Roe O'Neill and other leaders, fought many battles with varied success. After the death of Owen Roe, as it was believed by poison, and finding the Cromwellian party in England defeated, the Royalists and the Confederates broke up; and when Cromwell overran Ireland, the estates of the Royalists became the prey of his victorious army.

While the Parliament of England took no step to encourage loyal Irish to maintain the right of their king against his enemies, they made laws to destroy industry in Ireland. For this purpose the Act prohibiting the growth of tobacco in Ireland was passed, and more important merchandise was prohibited from being carried in Irish ships to the colonies. Restrictions were also placed on the number of sailors serving on board English ships, only a third of whom could be men of Ireland.

Though no Parliament met in Ireland during the time of Cromwell, Irish members were summoned to England, and attended the English Parliament. Care was taken that those members were of the party in rebellion against Charles I. They made no protest against the despoiling the estates of the loyal Irish who sat in the Confederate councils at Kilkenny, or fought under Owen Roe O'Neill, or other Irish generals, in many a hard-contested battle. While Richard Cromwell remained in Ireland as viceroy, he also sent Irish members of the same politics to the English House of Commons. On the Restoration the first Irish Parliament which met after the Cromwell era of twenty years was held in Chichester House, a large building on Corkhill, Dublin, with plenty of accommodation for Lords and Commons. Though Sir Maurice Eustace was lord chancellor, the Most Rev. John Bramhall, Archbishop of Armagh and Primate of all Ireland, was appointed by royal commission the Speaker of the House of Lords, and as such sat upon the woolsack. Sir Maurice Eustace, Roger Boyle, Earl of Orrery, and Charles Coote, Earl of Mountrath, lords justices, occupied seats elevated above the peers, over which was a canopy, as a symbol of state. Lord Baltinglas bore the sword of state, Viscount Montgomery the cap of maintenance, and the Earl of Kildare the robe.[1] To this Parliament only one Roman Catholic was returned, who, with an Anabaptist, was member for Trim. The Speaker of the House of Commons was Sir Audley Mervyn. In his inaugural address the Speaker noticed with approbation the exclusion of the Catholics: " I may warrantably say, since Ireland was happy under an English Government, there was never so choice a collection of Protestant fruit that ever grew within the walls of the Commons House. Your Lordships have piped in your summons to this Parliament, and the Irish have danced. How many have voted for and signed to the returns of Protestant elections? So that we may hope for, as we pray, that Japheth may be persuaded to dwell in the tent of Shem."[2]

By the death of Charles II. in 1685, without legitimate issue, his brother James, the Duke of York, was proclaimed king, under the title of James II. This, of course, caused much disgust to those

[1] *Lives of the Lord Chancellors of Ireland*, vol. i. p. 370.
[2] Gilbert's *History of Dublin*, vol. iii. p. 60.

who obtained the estates of the Catholics under the Act of Settlement, especially when they saw Roman Catholics appointed to the bench and other offices hitherto monopolised by Protestants. The change of the Duke of Tyrconnel for Lord Clarendon as lord-lieutenant, and Sir Alexander Fitton, Lord Gawsworth, for Sir Charles Porter as chancellor, increased the fears of the English party. These fears increased when it was known that, after leaving England, the king, queen, and their son sought and found refuge with Louis XIV., and that James II. was resolved to come as king to Ireland. His Majesty was loyally received in Cork in March 1688, and proceeded from Cork to Lismore Castle, thence to the Duke of Ormonde's castle at Kilkenny, and, amidst the rejoicings of the citizens, on Saturday, 24th March, entered Dublin in great state. The king lost no time in issuing a proclamation for assembling a Parliament in Dublin on May 7th. It is curious to remark that, on the Lords assembling, although there was a tolerably large attendance of Spiritual peers—six Protestant prelates—no Catholic bishops were summoned. One duke, ten earls, sixteen viscounts, twenty-one barons, with the six Spiritual peers, made fifty-four. These constituted the House of Lords, while the Commons sent two hundred and twenty-four members. They met at the King's Inns, and the king opened Parliament in person. This was the only time such an event occurred in Ireland. He wore his royal robes, and the Commons being summoned to the

House of Lords, his Majesty delivered the following speech from the throne:—

"My Lords and Gentlemen,— The exemplary loyalty which this nation hath expressed to me at a time when others of my subjects undutifully misbehaved themselves to me, or so basely deserted me, and your seconding my deputy, as you did, in his firm and resolute asserting my right, in preserving this kingdom for me, and putting it in a position of defence, made me resolve to come to you, and to venture my life with you in defence of your liberties and my own right. And to my great satisfaction I have not only found you ready to serve me, but that your courage has equalled your zeal. I have always been for liberty of conscience and against invading any man's property, having still in my mind the saying in Holy Writ: *Do as you would be done to, for that is the Law and the Prophets.*

"It was this liberty of conscience I gave which my enemies, both abroad and at home, dreaded, especially when they saw that I was resolved to have it established by law in all my dominions, and made them set themselves up against me, though for different reasons. Seeing that if I had once settled it, my people (in the opinion of the one) would have been too happy, and I (in the opinion of the other) too great. This argument was made use of to persuade their own people to join with them, and too many of my subjects to use me as they have done. But nothing shall ever persuade

me to change my mind as to that; and wheresoever
I am the master, I design (God willing) to establish
it by law, and to have no other test or distinction
but that of loyalty.

"I expect your concurrence in this Christian
work, and in making laws against profaneness
and all sorts of debauchery.

"I shall also most readily consent to the making
such good and wholesome laws as may be for the
general good of the nation, the improvement of trade,
and the relieving of such as have been injured by
the late Acts of Settlement, as far forth as may be
consistent with reason, justice, and the public good
of my people. And as I shall do my part to make
you happy and rich, I make no doubt of your assistance, by enabling me to oppose the unjust designs of
my enemies, and to make this nation flourish.

"And to encourage you the more to it, you know
with what ardour, generosity, and kindness the
Most Christian King gave a secure retreat to the
queen, my son, and myself, when we were forced
out of England, and came to seek for protection
and safety in his dominions; how he embraced my
interests, and gave me such supplies of all sorts
as enabled me to come to you, which, without his
obliging assistance, I could not have done; this he
did at a time when he had so many and so considerable enemies to deal with, and you see still
continues to do so.

"I shall conclude as I have begun, and assure
you I am as sensible as you can desire of the signal

loyalty you have expressed to me, and shall make it my chief study, as it has always been, to make you and all my subjects happy."[1]

The king having concluded his speech, the Lord Chancellor, Lord Gawsworth, desired the Commons to elect their Speaker. Their choice was Sir Richard Nagle, Attorney-General, a very able member of the Irish Bar. For the first time for many years the House of Commons, with six exceptions, was Roman Catholic, and Plowden says: "They were, perhaps, the fairest representatives of the people of Ireland ever sent to any Parliament in that kingdom."[2] We can very well imagine the anxiety with which those who, either by descent, by purchase, or by grants, held the forfeited estates, watched the course of events.

Only the titles of the Acts passed in this Parliament of King James II. were supposed to be preserved.[3] The Acts were publicly burnt, and a heavy penalty was to be imposed on any one preserving a copy. As I have procured the titles of these Acts, I give them here. The public can judge if they were deserving the censure so lavishly poured upon them.

1. An Act declaring that the Parliament of England cannot bind Ireland, and against writs of

---

[1] This speech is stated to be printed from an authentic copy in manuscript, sold by E. Rede, Dublin, in 1740.
[2] *Hist. Review*, vol. i. Appendix, p. 138.
[3] *Life and Death of the Irish Parliament.*

error and appeals to be brought, for removing judgments, decrees, and sentences in Ireland into England.

2. An Act for repealing the Acts of Settlement and Explanation.

3. An Act for taking off all incapacities of the natives of this kingdom.

4. An Act for repealing the Act for keeping and celebrating the 23rd of October as an anniversary thanksgiving in this kingdom.

5. An Act for liberty of conscience, and repealing such Acts and clauses in any Act of Parliament granted to his Grace James, Duke of Ormonde.

6. An Act for the encouragement of strangers and others to inhabit and plant in the kingdom of Ireland.

7. An Act prohibiting the importation of English, Scotch, or Welsh coals into this kingdom.

8. An Act for vesting in his Majesty the goods of absentees.

9. An Act for the advancement and improvement of trade, and for the encouragement and increasing shipping and navagation.

10. An Act for the attainder of divers rebels, and for the preserving the interests of loyal subjects.

We learn from the *Historical Review* by Dr. Ball, p. 271, in a very important note in the Appendix, that there were thirty-five Acts passed, so I have only named the principal. The note also gives the number of acres stated by Sir William Petty as having been restored to the original proprietors. He gives the entire number of Irish acres seized by the usurpers at 5,200,000. Of these, he says, the Roman Catholics got back 2,340,000. While the Protestants, in addition to the property of the Church, he estimates at 2,400,000 Irish acres. The remainder, 460,000 acres, were of course taken possession of by Cromwell's greedy soldiers; and while the families of the despoiled owners had the chance of recovering them, they got the lord chancellor to grant writs of restitution which authorised the sheriff to eject the intruders, and give back the lands to those who could prove their right to get them back. While Chief Justice Whiteside in our day, and Chief Justice Keating in 1689, considered these proceedings as unjust, because their lands had been acquired either by descent or purchase, and put into family settlements, surely both these learned judges must have been struck with the fact that those whose ancestors had been possessed of the lands for scores of years, and were only deprived of them by their loyalty, had every right to recover them when the turn of events gave them the power.

This power did not last long. William, Prince of Orange, who had married Mary, daughter of James II., was invited to England and made king. He was a brave general, and, invited to Ireland, fought the troops of James at the Boyne, Aughrim, and Athlone. Limerick capitulated, and it must be a reproach to the memory of King William III. that the articles of capitulation were violated.

As no Parliament was held in Ireland during the Jacobite and Williamite war, the English Parliament of 1690 annulled the Acts of the Irish Parliament of King James II.

Now it appears to me that several of these statutes were not only free from injustice and oppression, but likely to be beneficial. Yet they were denounced by no less an authority than the late Right Hon. James Whiteside, who, in reference to this Parliament, says: "This unjust Parliament, which King James packed through Tyrconnel's art, sat from 7th May till 20th June, and during that period contrived to perpetrate more acts of injustice and oppression than had ever been committed in the same space of time by any legislative assembly in the world." He refers to Archbishop King's work, entitled *The State of the Protestants in Ireland under the late King James' Government*—a work written solely from a most prejudiced point of view, and which the eminent prelate wrote before the natural emtions of joy and exultation for conquest over those who had sat in King James' Parliament had time to cool. His party contended James was not king when he convened this Parliament.[1]

---

[1] I am glad to find my opinion of the much-abused Parliament of King James II. sustained by very good politicians and historians. In the very able work, *Young Ireland*, published by Sir Charles Gavan Duffy, when referring to the contributions of Davis to the *Citizen Magazine*, Sir Charles says: "The Irish Parliament of James II., which has been systematically

That the English Convention Parliament of 1688 had conferred the Crown of England, Ireland, and Scotland on William and Mary; while on the other side the legality of this Parliament was asserted. It was urged that three constitutional bodies were present—King, Lords, and Commons. That the Commons were duly elected by writs directed to the proper returning officer. The peers summoned, and both Spiritual and Temporal Lords sat in the usual way. Five new creations of peers were, according to Mr. Lynch in his *Legal Institutions*, made legally and in order.

misrepresented, he made the subject of a careful review, and printed several of its Acts *in extenso*, to vindicate its moderate and practical character."

Mr. Lecky, the distinguished author, in a note in *The History of England in the Eighteenth Century*, expresses a hope that the notices of James's Parliament should be republished. Davis contemplated doing so, entitling the work *The Patriot Parliament*, 1689, *with the Statutes, Biographical Notices of King, Lords, and Commons*, etc., edited by Thomas Davis, Barrister-at-Law.

CHAPTER IX.

1690–1713.

Lord Sydney, Viceroy—Parliament in 1692—Oath excluding Catholics—Viceroy desires to maintain the Treaty of Limerick—Lord Chancellor Sir Constantine Phipps censured by the House of Commons—Defended by the House of Lords—Difference between Lord Chancellor Cox and Privy Council.

SHORTLY after the arrival of Lord Sydney as viceroy in 1692, a Parliament met in Dublin. As the members, both Lords and Commons, were required to take the oath of supremacy enacted during the reign of Queen Elizabeth, no Catholic could take this oath. In neither the House of Lords nor Commons was any Catholic present. Considerable difference existed between the lord-deputy and the Parliament. The Irish House of Commons insisted on its exclusive right to originate money bills, which the viceroy wished to obtain. When the Irish Parliament asserted their independence, much discussion thus arose respecting the breach of the Treaty of Limerick, and it was asserted that some changes had been introduced after the treaty was signed. There were some efforts made to prevent

Catholics being allowed to make claims, and discussion ensued between the Chancellor and the Speaker of the House of Commons.

The viceroy, Earl of Pembroke, opened Parliament on 7th July 1707, and the concluding words of his speech were these:—" My Lords and Gentlemen, In order to the attaining and establishing the safety and welfare of this kingdom, I shall think myself extremely happy if, during my administration, all matters should be conducted with that temper and prudence as may justly entitle you to the countenance of her Majesty's affections. For my own part, though a great honour to serve in this post, I can profess no satisfaction in it without your happiness and prosperity, the which I shall sincerely endeavour to promote; and hope, but chiefly by your assistance, to secure the good of this kingdom, and show in our several stations that we are united in our affections to each other, as well as in duty to the best of queens."

Those good intentions of his excellency were insufficient to control the intolerant spirit of the age. Strong remonstrances from the Roman Catholics, who had been dispossessed of their estates by the Act of Settlement and Explanation, had the effect of causing some attention being given to their case. A Court was ordered to be held, but only for a very limited time. By its short sitting and abrupt termination, over three thousand claims were shut out; yet this limited justice actually so frightened the Puritan settlers that they formed a conspiracy to seize the Castle of Dublin, and induced several members of the Irish Parliament to join the plot. The castle was to be seized on the 11th May 1663. The viceroy (Duke of Ormonde), when aware of the conspiracy, took prompt action, and defeated the design. Four of the leaders were hanged, and this sufficed to break it up. Another plot of the Puritans, in 1671, also was discovered in time to be frustrated.

Of course, in this Parliament, where only one Catholic was returned when the Acts of Settlement and Explanation were passed,[1] the Catholic owners had no voice. These Acts carried out the provisions of the Act passed in England under the title of the Adventure Act, and restored the estates of the Catholics and Protestants who had remained faithful to the father of King Charles II., and hoped on his restoration to be restored to the properties of which they had been deprived by their fidelity to Charles I.; but the king, finding the Cromwellian interest in Ireland too strong, did not attempt to do justice to the Catholics of Ireland. Thus it was that Cromwell's partisans had their own way over Ireland. While the forfeited estates of the so-called rebels were being disposed of, the Cromwellian claimants for these estates sent as an agent to London, to get them as they expected, the Right Rev. Dr. Boyle, Lord Bishop of Cork. Through his influence with the English Privy

---

[1] Statutes 14 and 15 Charles II. chap. 2; and 17 and 18 Charles II. chap. 2.

Council, he secured large grants for his party; and though the Irish, who knew they were to be despoiled, also sent some gentlemen to act in their behalf, the bishop had sufficient influence to have them kept aloof from the Privy Council, and they were stigmatised as "the Potato Ambassadors."

Having triumphed completely over the Irish Royalists, the dominant faction were not slow to reward the bishop. By his exertions, Cromwell's soldiers, besides sharing the distribution of a large sum of money, although in fact many had fought against, and not for, Charles I., the claims of the Irish Catholics were postponed until those who were in possession of the estates were fully repaid their advances in money, or for their arrears of pay.

On the 24th May 1662 it was ordered by the Lords Spiritual and Temporal in the present Parliament assembled, that the memorial of thanks to the Lord Bishop of Cork for his services performed in England, be entered in the journal of this House, *in hæc verba.*

Upon a report made this day by the Lord Viscount Conway and Lord Viscount Massareene unto this House, of the ample, clear, and undoubted testimony which his Majesty's lords justices of Ireland have received of the great and eminent services performed both to his Majesty and this kingdom by the right rev. father in God, Michael Boyle, Lord Bishop of Cork, in the late trust he was employed about in England, concerning the Bill for the settlement of Ireland, which hath been eminently carried on and managed by his presence, virtue, and indefatigable endeavours: It is ordered that the said lord bishop, for his effectual endeavours in accomplishing that service, which was committed unto him by the lords justices and Council, in reference to the good and settlement of this kingdom, be entered in the journal book of this House, together with the lords justices' recommendation, to remain to posterity as a mark of honour and testimony of the gratitude of the House to the said Lord Bishop of Cork.[1] He had something more satisfactory in £1000 from the king, and large grants under the Act of Settlement.[2]

An English statute, called the Adventure Act, created great offence in Ireland. It was passed really to grant the forfeited lands of the alleged disloyal Irish to such adventurers as would pay into the English treasury money to give pay to the soldiers employed in suppressing the so-called rebellion of 1641. At this time the Confederate Catholics held a council at Kilkenny, which resembled the appearance of a Parliament. It was held on 24th October 1642. There were eleven Spiritual and fourteen Temporal peers, and twenty-six representative commoners. A Speaker presided, and twenty-four members of supreme council, six from each province, peers and commons, sat in one chamber, not a separate one, but prepared for the

---

[1] *Lords' Jour. Ir.* vol. i. p. 302.
[2] *Lives of the Lord Chancellors,* vol. i. p. 395.

Lords when in consultation. Lord Mountgarett was elected president of the supreme council.[1]

Besides, the penal commercial customs and navigation restrictions impeded Irish commerce. Not more than one-fourth could be Irishmen on board merchant ships. Importation of cattle or provisions from Ireland was not allowed. Such was the state of the navigation laws, that a ship from an English settlement in America, with colonial produce, was stranded on the Irish coast, the law did not allow the cargo to be landed in Ireland, or to be removed in an Irish ship. An English ship had to be sent for, and although the cargo was required in the Irish market, it could not be delivered in Ireland, without being again re-shipped to Ireland.[2]

It was the Parliament of William and Mary in England that annulled all the statutes passed in the Irish Parliament of King James II. When the Irish Parliament met in 1695, it was occupied with the impeachment of the lord chancellor, Sir Charles Porter, who was charged with taking excessive fees, with favouring Papists against Protestants, and acting partially on various occasions.

Having obtained permission to be allowed to speak in his own defence in the House of Commons, he was allowed to do so, and his defence was so complete, that, on the question put, it was held sufficient without going into any evidence. The chancellor's acquittal was carried in the affirmative

---

[1] Rev. T. O'Hanlon, *Catechism of Irish History*, p. 378.
[2] *Huckman's Speeches*, vol. iii. p. 9.

by a considerable majority, the numbers being 121 for, to 77 against, the chancellor.

The Speaker, Rochfort, was much upset at the triumph of the chancellor; and was returning home, when, in Essex Street, Dublin, while the Speaker's coach was proceeding through that narrow thoroughfare, another coach endeavoured to pass. This coach contained Sir Charles Porter, the lord chancellor, also homeward bound. The anger of the Speaker, excited by the triumph of the chancellor in the House of Commons, was rekindled by the chancellor's coachman trying to pass, and, letting down the window of his coach, he desired the chancellor's coachman to keep back. Finding this order unheeded, the Speaker at once leaped from his carriage, seized the reins of the chancellor's horses, and nearly brought them down. He then directed the Speaker's mace, which was in his coach, to be brandished in the face of the astonished coachman of the chancellor, declaring he would be run down by his man, and would justify what he did. The chancellor's coachman then allowed the Speaker's coach to proceed without further interruption. Next day the lord chancellor brought the matter under the consideration of the peers, alleging the conduct of the Speaker of the House of Commons was an insult to him as Speaker of the House of Lords; but their lordships considered the chance meeting of the coaches in a narrow street could not be regarded as a premeditated insult, and the affair was allowed to drop.

I quite agree with my friend, the late Daniel Owen Maddon, when he says: "To rake up past history for materials to exasperate the politics of the present time is a hateful practice, worthy only of a heartless demagogue or an extravagant fanatic. But there are occasions when it is useful to reflect upon the enormities of the past. And when wonder is expressed why the social state of Ireland is so calamitous, let the history of the country from 1688 to 1829 be examined, and it will appear evident to any impartial or judicious inquirer, that it is unreasonable to expect deep-seated evils can be removed in a single generation, even by the wisest laws or the most skilful statesmen. The operation of the Revolution of 1688, so beneficial to England and to mankind, was ruinous to Ireland."

CHAPTER X.

1706–1713.

On the Mode prescribed to appoint a Lord Justice—Statute 33 Henry VIII.—Contradictory Opinions thereon—How disposed of—Parliament of 1707—the Viceroy's Conciliatory Address.

On the 28th January 1706, while the viceroy, the Duke of Ormonde, was absent in London, and the lord chancellor, Sir Richard Cox, and Lord Cutts, commander-in-chief, were lords justices, Lord Cutts died suddenly.

By statute 33 Henry VIII., on the avoidance of every the king's lieutenant, deputy, or justices of the realm, by death, surrender, or departure out of the realm, it was required that the chancellor should write to the king's counsellors to elect a governor, and upon the election he should seal letters patent; and such person being sworn, should have the same authority as the king, lieutenant, or deputy then next before him used to have, until the king do admit and authorise one to be his lieutenant or governor, and until he be sworn as accustomed.

Having met the Privy Council at the Castle, the

lord chancellor requested their advice, which was that he should send writs, and proceed to a new election; and those most ready for this course declared their readiness to elect him sole governor, as had been done a few years previously, when, on the death of the viceroy, Lord Capel, the then chancellor, Sir Charles Porter, had been elected sole lord justice. The chancellor, it seems, had a suspicion that these advisers would not scruple to mislead, and expressed his doubts as to the propriety of this course. He considered the statute of Henry VIII. referred to head governor, and that he had no right to assume a power not warranted by the statute. The chancellor consulted precedents,—that most in point, when the viceroy, Earl of Strafford, was a prisoner in the Tower, and the Lord Justice Wandesford died, the council did not proceed to a new election, but used the words, "*that the Government was unsupplied.*" The chancellor then consulted the judges and law officers, who thought with the chancellor that writs ought not to be issued. The queen and her legal adviser in England also held the chancellor was right. The Duke of Ormonde was removed from the office of viceroy, and the chancellor with the primate, by letters patent dated 16th February 1706, were appointed lords justices. But this refusal of the lord chancellor to proceed with the election was the ground of a resolution of the House of Commons, for the House resolved—1st, That by the death of Lord Cutts, on 26th January

1706, the kingdom became destitute of a governor residing in the same until 15th February following. 2nd, That no writ was issued by Sir Richard Cox, lord chancellor, for electing a justice pursuant to the statute of 33 Henry VIII. from 26th January to 15th February 1706, at which time the primate and lord chancellor were constituted lords justices under the Great Seal. 3rd, That it was, and is, the indispensable duty of the lord chancellor or lord keeper, when the kingdom is destitute, to issue writs to summon the privy councillors to elect a chief governor pursuant to the statute of Henry VIII.[1] These resolutions being affirmed by the precedents, ten of the judges, the law officers of England and Ireland, the ex-chancellor did not suffer in his reputation, and no action was taken on the resolutions of the House of Commons.

[1] *Lives of Lord Chancellors*, vol. i. p. 525.

CHAPTER XI.

1713-1759.

Anecdote of Addison—Parliament in 1713—George I.—The Court of Appeal—Statute 6 George I. to bind Ireland—Effect of Statute of William III.—Depressed Irish Trade—Dean Swift's Advice—Legend of Minerva and Arachne—Wood's Coinage—The Drapier's Letters—The Irish Club—A Satire on the House of Lords.

IT appears that during this session, Addison, then secretary to the viceroy and member for Cavan, showed how sometimes the gift of public speaking was wanting to the literary genius. It also happens that the gifted orator is by no means a ready writer, and this is instanced in the case of Henry Grattan. Addison having risen in the House to address the Irish Commons, had only said, " I conceive, Sir," when he was mute. After a brief pause he again said, " Mr. Speaker, I conceive," when he found himself wholly unable to continue. Cries of " Hear! hear!" brought him again on his legs, when he repeated, " I conceive, Sir," and was once more at a loss how to proceed. He sat down amid stifled merriment, which broke forth into shouts of laughter when an honourable member said, "Sir, the member for Cavan has conceived three times, but brought forth *nothing*."

It is seldom any good deed is attributed to the Earl of Wharton, but his selection of Mr. Brodrick to succeed Sir Richard Pyne as Chief Justice of the Queen's Bench in 1719, is instanced as a good deed. "He obtained that high post for one of the most worthy patriots of that kingdom as an instance of the care he took of the security of religion and liberty."[1]

Mr. Brodrick was then knighted, and, as Chief Justice of the Queen's Bench, called to the Upper House. On leaving the Commons on 20th May 1709, the following resolution was adopted:—"That the thanks of this House be given to the Right Honourable Alan Brodrick, late Speaker of this House, and now Lord Chief Justice of her Majesty's Court of Queen's Bench, for his faithful and eminent services performed to this House, in the Chair, and during the time of his being Speaker;" and the Lord Mayor and Mr. Serjeant Caulfield were ordered to attend his lordship and acquaint him with the vote of thanks of the House.[2]

So high a compliment could not fail of being very acceptable. The reply of the chief justice was as follows:—"I am extremely sensible of this great honour done me, as I always have been of the goodness of the House of Commons in supporting me in the discharge of the trust they were

---

[1] *Life of the Earl of Wharton.*
[2] *Com. Jour. Ir.* vol. ii. p. 644.

pleased to repose in me; and I can't sufficiently acknowledge their favour, or express the satisfaction I feel, that the witnesses of my behaviour during so many sessions of Parliament have unanimously approved of it, and given an uncontrovertible testimony of my having, in all instances, to the best of my power, done my duty to the Crown, the House of Commons, and the kingdom in England."[1]

The separation between him and his brother members in the Commons was not of long duration. At this time the judges held their seats at the king's, or rather the ministers' pleasure, and a change of administration having occurred shortly after this, the ministry deprived Sir Alan Brodrick of the chief justiceship of the Queen's Bench, to make room for Sir Robert Cox. A dissolution of Parliament took place on 6th May 1713, and new writs being issued, Sir Alan Brodrick was returned one of the knights of the shire of Cork. The Duke of Shrewsbury opened the new Parliament on the 25th November following; and the Commons having re-elected their former Speaker, in the course of the usual speech announcing this fact, the Speaker shortly, but clearly, defines the duties of the office. "To collect readily the true sense of a numerous assembly, to form the same into questions, in order to their final resolution, and to present their conclusions, declarations, and petitions to your Grace in the best manner, and with full advantage, is part of the duty which that man undertakes who is hardy

[1] *Com. Jour. Ir.* vol. ii. p. 647.

enough to accept so ordinary a province; and the sense I have of my own imperfections and disabilities makes me tremble when I reflect on the difficulties under which learned, experienced, and wise men have laboured in the Chair of that House. But when I consider that my endeavours to serve her Majesty and this kingdom in the Chair of a former Parliament were so acceptable to, and approved by, the whole House of Commons, that they were pleased to express their sense of them by a signal mark of their respect, after I had ceased to be a member of their House; when I consider that, out of many gentlemen of great abilities and knowledge in the laws and methods of Parliament, the Commons have now again judged me capable of filling the Chair to their expectation, I have not put my own fears and diffidence of myself in balance with their superior judgment."

He then went on to express strong hopes of unanimity, and that the warmest contest might be who should show most zeal in duty to the queen, adherence to the constitution in Church and State, and useful to the viceroy's person and government.[1]

The chancellor, Sir Constantine Phipps, and the Speaker, were at this time very bitter foes, so the chancellor merely informed the Speaker in very curt terms "that the viceroy acquiesced in the choice of the House of Commons." Sir Alan Brodrick was not long left in the Chair. On the death of Queen Anne, George I. became King of

[1] *Com. Jour. Ir.* vol. ii. p. 747.

Great Britain and Ireland, and one of his first acts was to create Sir Alan Brodrick Lord Chancellor of Ireland, with the title of Viscount Middleton. He was blamed for not influencing his son, a member of Parliament, to support the Government, who desired to repeal the Test Act, which his son stoutly opposed. Yet such conduct deserves praise, not blame. I find, in an article on the "Peels of Manchester,"[1] the first Sir Robert Peel intimated difference of opinion between him and his gifted son, the second Sir Robert, on the subject of the Currency Bill. In presenting a petition signed by many leading merchants of London, praying the rejection of the Bill introduced by his son, Sir Robert said: "To-night I shall have to oppose a very near and dear relation; but while it is my own sentiment that I have a duty to perform, I respect those who do theirs, and who consider that duty to be paramount to all other considerations."

The son in reply was equally graceful. Referring to the difficulties which he had to encounter in bringing forward his measure, he remarked: "Not the least is one which it pains me to observe—I mean the necessity I am under of opposing myself to an authority to which I have always bowed from my youth upward, and to which I hope I shall always continue to bow with deference. My excuse now is, that I have a great public duty imposed upon me, and that whatever may be my private feeling, from that duty I must not shrink."

[1] *London Society*, vol. ix. p. 175.

While Sir Ralph Gore was Speaker, he was appointed one of the lords justices in the absence of the viceroy, Lord Carteret, in 1730, and a reprieve he granted gave rise to a curious question of criminal law.

On the death of Queen Anne, the House of Hanover supplied a monarch for Great Britain and Ireland in the person of George I. At this time the relations of the Parliament of Great Britain and Ireland were not friendly. The difference respecting the House of Lords as the Court of Ultimate Appeal in legal matters was marked. While the English lords considered they were to decide, the Irish lords, acting on the opinion of the Irish judges, held they, and they alone, could decide on cases of appeal from the Irish Courts. The English Parliament resolved to teach the Irish lords a lesson. So by statute 6 George I. it was made law, that not only was the House of Lords in England the Court of Ultimate Appeal in all cases tried in the Irish Courts, but that the Parliament of Great Britain had full power to make laws binding on the people of Ireland, because the Parliament of Ireland was subordinate to the Parliament of England.

While the Parliament of Great Britain was thus asserting its superiority over Ireland, this country was hampered by the shackles upon her trade, effected by the Acts of William III. No doubt these Acts were pressed at the instance of English traders, but some regard ought to have been shown to Ireland, which was then consigned to a terrible state of poverty and want.

The statutes of William III., which destroyed the woollen manufacture of Ireland, and the restrictions on Irish navigation, induced Dean Swift to make a vigorous effort to arouse a regard for national industry in Ireland. He accordingly published "a proposal for the universal use of Irish manufactures in cloth and furniture of houses, utterly refusing and renouncing everything wearable which comes from England." He mentions the saying of some person who suggested to Dr. Vesey, Archbishop of Tuam, that everything that came from England should be burned, except the people and the coals." The dean would prefer the people staying in their own country, and the coal mines of Ireland made more productive. Ovid's legend of Minerva and Arachne seemed to the dean so *apropos* to the state of England and Ireland, that he referred to how the goddess Minerva, hearing the great fame of the spinster Arachne, resolved on a contest as to which could best spin. On the trial of skill, the goddess, jealous of her rival, condemned her to become a spider, and to be perpetually spinning from her own bowels. The dean considered Ireland much worse treated than Arachne, because the woollen substance of the bowels of Ireland was absorbed by England without being allowed to weave or spin. When the reign of George II. commenced in great hostility to the English Government, this monarch had granted a patent for the coinage of copper money to an ironmonger of Wolverhampton named Wood. This patent being granted, the money coined without reference to the Irish Parliament, causing national resentment, and the money being regarded as inferior, made all classes in Ireland refuse its circulation. The attempt to circulate Wood's coinage caused Dean Swift to write the celebrated Drapier's Letters. Not content with denouncing Wood and his money, the dean, in his fourth letter, argued that the kingdom of Ireland was quite as independent of England as England was of Ireland. He referred to Molyneux as a greater authority, and the power of the Drapier Letters caused such a spirit of discontent against the Government, instructions were given to prosecute the printer, on the ground the letters tended to stir up enmity between England and Ireland. Public feeling, however, defeated the effort. Though Chief Justice Whitshed made every effort to induce the grand jury of the city of Dublin to find a bill of indictment, they refused to do so, and therefore there was no criminal trial. An attempt, however, was made to suppress the Drapier Letters; for though they were published anonymously, the dean was supposed to be the author, and became the idol of the people. The Duke of Grafton, then viceroy, and the Irish executive resolved to prosecute the printer, and Whitshed, Chief Justice of the King's Bench, presided at the trial of Waters, the printer, and sent back the jury *nine times*, in order to make them, if possible, return a verdict of guilty.

They would not do so. By way of a compromise between the arbitrary conduct of the chief justice and their consciences, they found a special verdict; and the viceroy, on receiving instructions from England, directed the attorney-general to enter a *noli prosequi*, and Waters was no further tried. The dean is always regarded as a true patriot, and should we have our Irish Parliament restored, I hope his advice respecting the use of Irish manufactured goods may be acted on. I also hope the essays of Thomas Davis may be followed, as they contain most excellent suggestions for the youth of Ireland.

The dean evidently refers to the prosecution of the printer in his satire on the House of Lords:

> "Ye paltry underlings of state,
> Ye senators who love to prate,
> Ye rascals of inferior note,[1]
> Who for a dinner sell a vote;[1]
> Ye pack of pensionary peers,
> Whose fingers itch for poet's ears;
> Ye bishops, far removed from saints,
> Why all this rage? why these complaints?
> Why against printers all this noise,
> This summoning of blackguard boys?
> Take my advice to make you safe,
> I know a shorter way by half.
> The point is plain, remove the cause,
> Defend your liberties and laws.
> Be sometimes to your country true,
> Have once the public good in view;
> Bravely despise champagne at court,
> And choose to dine at home with port;

---

[1] Evidently alluding to the recent statute 6 Geo. I.

> Let prelates, by their good behaviour,
> Convince us they believe a Saviour ;
> Nor sell what they so dearly bought,
> This country, now their own, for nought.
> Ne'er did a true satiric muse
> Virtue or innocence abuse ;
> And 'tis against poetic rules
> To rail at men by nature fools."

Having thus lashed the peers, the House of Commons received a touch of the same brush:

> "As I stroll the city, oft I
> Spy a building large and lofty,
> Not a bow-shot from the College,
> Half the globe from sense and knowledge."

The Parliament House on College Green was only the space of Westmoreland Street from Trinity College, Dublin.

The venality of the members was such as to merit this reproach :

> "In the porch Briareus stands,
> Shows a bribe in all his hands ;
> Briareus the Secretary,
> But we mortals call him Carey ;
> When the rogues their country fleece,
> They may hope for pence a-piece."

The office of secretary to the viceroy was no sinecure. While in the reign of George II. it endangered the life of the holder, in our day his conduct is usually sharply criticised in the questions put in the Imperial Parliament.

This will appear in my next chapter, when an Irish riot of unexampled duration, in Ireland, took place. It may be as memorable in Irish annals as the Porteous riot in Edinburgh, or the Gordon riots in London; and it shows that, as we scan Ireland, the Irish aristocracy of peers and members of the House of Commons favoured the union with the Parliament of Great Britain. The Irish people sturdily opposed it.

During the reign of Queen Anne we find the desire for a union announced by the Irish Lords and Commons. A resolution passed by the Lords on 25th October 1703 is to desire that Queen Anne might qualify that Ireland should be represented in England; and in 1707, in an address from the Irish House of Commons congratulating the queen on the union with Scotland, the Irish House of Commons prayed that God might put it into her Majesty's heart to add greater strength and lustre to her crown by a yet more comprehensive union. But the notion of a union with Ireland was not well received in England. So many Scotch adventurers had made good their hold on English soil, the English had no desire that a like importation from Ireland should occur. Though a desire for union was then shown by the Irish Parliament, it was not favoured by the Irish people. Considerable jealousy prevailed at this time as to the claim asserted by the English House of Lords to be the Court of Ultimate Appeal from Irish as well as English trials.[1]

[1] *Lords' Journal*, ii. 29 ; *Commons' Journal*, 20th October 1707.

In 1713, the lord chancellor, Sir Constantine Phipps, having incurred the displeasure of the House of Commons, by absenting himself when lord justice from the Orange body, who, on the anniversary of the landing of King William III. in Ireland, were accustomed to display their respect for the victor of the Boyne, by surrounding his statue in College Green, and showing a friendly feeling towards the Catholics, had a resolution condemning his action and a complaint made to Queen Anne on his partial conduct.

But the House of Lords and the corporation of Bandon most vigorously defended the chancellor, and the complimentary language of the House of Lords and the death of Queen Anne left the chancellor able to relinquish a position which afforded him no peace of mind. He was succeeded in his office of lord chancellor of Ireland by an excellent lawyer, Sir Richard Cox. He had not been long in office before an incident occurred which brought his legal skill into requisition.

CHAPTER XII.

1759–1760.

Anti-Union Riot in Dublin—Peers compelled to swear against a Union—The Desire in the House—Danger of the *Commons' Journal*—Ireland to hang the Secretary—No Action by the Lord Mayor—No Riot Act in Ireland—The Viceroy calls out the Military—Humane Commander-in-Chief—Loss of Life before Mob dispersed—The King indignant—The Secretary gives a Convivial Party—Has to give an Explanation.

THE gentle dulness of the Lords was rudely broken in 1759, during the viceroyalty of the Duke of Bedford. A rumour spread through the city that a union was contemplated between Great Britain and Ireland, and was to be brought forward in the Irish Parliament. This caused the most intense excitement in the Irish metropolis, and the citizens of Dublin arose *en masse* to signify their hostility to the proposed measure. In order to allay their wrath, Mr. Rigby, secretary to the viceroy, addressed them, and declared "there were no grounds whatever for their apprehensions." This assurance having failed to dispel the idea, the Speaker, the Right Hon. John Ponsonby, son of the

Earl of Bessborough, relying on his popularity and that of his family, said the same, but with no better success. The people were fearfully excited; they seized many of the Lords on their way to the Parliament House, and obliged them to swear "fidelity to Ireland," and that they would vote against the union. Lord Inchiquin was one of the first met. The mob pulled off his periwig and red ribbon, and as he had a great impediment in his speech, which they attributed to disinclination to take their pledge, one official cried out, " D——n you, why do you hesitate?" Luckily, he was recognised as the chief of the O'Briens of Thomond, and then, with the greatest respect, they replaced his hat, wig, and ribbon, and cheered him on his way. They then caught the Bishop of Killala, whom they made get out of his coach and take the oath. Lord Bowes, lord chancellor, came next. His carriage was stayed, and he tendered the oath, whereat he grew very indignant, but, regarding discretion as the better part of valour, he complied, and then was compelled to repeat it in the presence of Lord Chief Justice Caulfield, the mob considering the presence of the chief justice giving greater efficacy to the oath. The chancellor and chief justice were then allowed to pass on. Several peers, who contrived to get into the Lords unmolested, were proceeding with formal business, Lord Farnham was taking the customary oath on taking his seat on the death of his father on 6th August 1759, when the rabble entered the House of Lords, and insisted upon Lord Farnham taking their oath also. The rioters then indulged in all sorts of outrageous conduct. They dragged a feeble old woman into the House from College Green, and placed her on the throne, put a pipe in her mouth, and insisted on her smoking. Having satisfied their spirit for mischief in the Lords, they rushed in hundreds into the House of Commons, and were about to burn the journals and documents of that assembly, when some one proposed "they should hang Rigby," recently appointed master of the rolls. The object of popular fury, probably expecting personal outrage, prudently kept out of harm's way, so they were not able to effect their purpose. During these riotous proceedings, the authorities were consulting how to quell the outbreak. The lord-lieutenant sent an express to the lord mayor, John Tew, calling on him to preserve the peace of the city. Lord Mayor Tew returned for answer, "that he could do nothing, for there was *no Riot Act in Ireland!*" Then the Privy Council, such as were within summons, met, and the commander-in-chief, General John Leslie, eighth Earl of Rothes, K.T., received orders from the viceroy, as general governor of the kingdom, to put down the riot by force of arms.

This brave and humane officer took the troops out, and ordered the cavalry to ride among the crowd and try and disperse them, using their sabres only, and no firearms. Yet such was the obstinacy of the mob, that before peace was restored, no fewer than sixteen of the rioters lost their lives. These scandalous proceedings called forth prompt action. The day following this tumult, the Commons resolved, "That assaulting, insulting, or menacing any member of their House, on his coming to or from it, or on account of his behaviour in Parliament, was a high infringement on their privileges, a most outrageous and dangerous violation of the rights of Parliament, and a high crime and misdemeanour."

A committee was selected to inquire and report as to the persons implicated in the riot, and to prepare an address to his Excellency to thank him for his energy in causing the dispersion of the rioters, and requesting him to offer a reward for the discovery of the guilty persons or their abettors. The House then called the corporation before them. The lord mayor and sheriffs were summoned to the Bar, and admonished by the Speaker, who censured them for not obeying the order to keep the avenues to the House free and open, and for permitting these riotous assemblages. Nor were the Lords behindhand. An address from their lordships was presented by the lord chancellor to the viceroy, thanking him for his seasonable interposition in having made use of the most effectual means for dispersing a most dangerous and insolent multitude of persons assembled before the Parliament House, in order most illegally and audaciously to obstruct and insult the members of both Houses of Parliament attending the public service of the nation, in manifest violation of the rights and privileges of Parliament.

The king (George II.) was quite indignant at what he regarded as the gross supineness of the civic authorities of Dublin, and desired "that an inquiry should take place by the executive as to what course should be taken to punish them."

Some curious illustrations of the habits of Peers and Commons during the last century may relieve the dry details of the transactions of the Irish Parliament. The secretary Rigby, whose narrow escape from popular violence, in consequence of his suspected design to promote the union between Great Britain and Ireland, appears to have been a great promoter of the excessive drinking prevalent during the last century. The quantity of liquor consumed at Rigby's banquets, and the excesses committed thereat, caused the wine-bibbing secretary to be censured by the less convivial members of the Government in England; and Sir Robert Wilmot, who was chief of the Irish department in London, on hearing of some breach of the temperance laws, wrote sharply in reference to this case. Rigby thus excused himself: "Now for the drunken story. It is very certain Mr. Pery and I once dined together since I came to Ireland, and it is true that we liked one another well enough not to part till near three in the morning, long before which time the company was reduced to a *tête-à-tête*, except one other drunk and asleep in a corner of the room. Who, therefore, had been accurate enough to remember the whole conversation, I cannot imagine, but you may assure yourself their ingenuity much exceeds their veracity. I have never heard or seen any symptoms of anger from Kildare [1] or Malone [2] from that night's jollity till I read it in your letter this morning. We both, I believe, made free with the times, as people in high spirits and in their cups are apt to do; but I really believe, were I to show it to him, Pery would be as much surprised as I am, to hear that our fun was made matter for serious discourse or deliberation. I am much obliged to you, Sir Robert, for sending me all these stories; I am as much entertained, and can laugh at them more than those that invent them. I know that a secretary is lawful game for everybody to fly at, and I should be very sorry to have led so insipid a life as to be suffered to pass unenvied, and consequently uncensured, through that employment. Let me hear from you, the oftener the better; and when, from Parliament and claret, from councils and bumpers, I can find time to work, I shall think my time well bestowed in answering you." [3]

The small attendance, and equally small amount of work, in the House of Lords at this time formed

[1] This was James, twentieth Earl of Kildare. He was created Marquis of Kildare in 1760, and Duke of Leinster in 1766. He built Leinster House, Dublin.

[2] Right Hon. Anthony Malone, one of the most eminent members of the Irish Bar, and one of the greatest ornaments of the House of Commons.

[3] *Bedford Correspondence*, Introduction iii. p. 23.

a strong contrast with that of the Irish House of Commons. Seldom above thirty peers, and of these were about a dozen bishops, would drop in to the Lords. The business was of a very trivial nature. Preparing addresses to the Crown or viceroy, introducing new peers to the House, occasional debates on some question from the Commons, constituted the chief matters recorded in the *Lords' Journals*. Rigby complained: " I am kept every day in the House of Commons till six or seven o'clock on one nonsensical motion or another. I am railed at by one party for being the mover of all these inflammatory inquiries, and the great incendiary; and the other condemning me for my candour and good-humour towards (for they would not have me speak to) any that vote against the Castle." [1]

At this time a great effort was made by the Government to deprive the Irish House of Commons of the right to initiate money bills, and the viceroy canvassed all the officials to influence them on this subject.

The postmaster-general gave a timid and irresolute reply. He declared: "Should an adjournment be proposed for a week, or a longer time, he would certainly vote against it." Most of the junior officers, as might be expected, were under the necessity of supporting the viceroy, but their votes were of no avail. The national sentiment was all-powerful. On the division postponing the Money Bill, the votes were 85 for, to 64 against,

[1] *Vide Correspondence of the Duke of Bedford*, vol. ii.

—a majority against the Government of 21. This made the viceroy very indignant. He complained "that officers in the army, in the revenue, nay, what caused him still greater surprise, commissioners of various public departments, who dipped very freely into the king's purse, voted against the king's ministers." To the annoyance of Rigby and the viceroy, the success of this vote caused some bold spirits to question the policy of being confined and impeded by Poynings' Law. It was with a fixed purpose of undermining the growing progress of patriotic ardour, Rigby gave a succession of dinner parties, where the utmost mirth and hilarity prevailed.

The habits of the Irish gentry at this period were of a nature to render these ministerial banquets quite consonant to their tastes. Hard drinking was the vice of the upper classes, and, as the example was one sure to find imitators, we cannot feel much surprised if it spread so extensively amongst the lower classes, that I have heard the existence of spontaneous combustion doubted, for it was said, "had it existed, the people of Ireland would be *off in a blaze.*"

CHAPTER XIII.

1760-1767.

Protestant Parliamentary Patriots—Lucas, Flood, Grattan, and Burgh—Charles Lucas born 1713, died 1771—Makes Charges in Supply of Drugs—Publishes "Pharmacomastrix"—In 1741 Lucas a Town Councillor—Corporation Question decided in favour of the Aldermen of Dublin—Sends Charter to the King with Account of the Citizens being robbed of their Rights—The Lords Justices decline to send to the King—In 1733 Lucas elected Member for the City of Dublin—Directs strict Obedience to Laws in after years O'Connell declared—In 1749 the House of Commons declares Lucas an Enemy to his Country—His Conduct when arrested—Imprisoned in Newgate—The cruel Order for his Treatment in Prison induces him to Escape—Dr. Johnson's Opinion in his Favour.

BEFORE proceeding with my account of the events which followed the accession of George III. to the British throne in 1760, I wish to make my readers acquainted with some of the great men whose devotion to Ireland procured her legislative independence. They were one and all Protestants, because the unjust penal laws barred the path of Roman Catholics to Parliament. Some had passed away—Dean Swift, whose Drapier's Letters fanned the sparks.

One of the most remarkable members of the Irish House of Commons during the eighteenth century was Charles Lucas, M.D., whose courage, honesty, and boldness in asserting the rights and liberties of Ireland, obtained for him the proud title of the "Incorruptible Lucas." Like Aristides in Greece, and Fabricius in Rome, he was tempted, but his pure heart refused to listen to the voice of the seducer, and he preferred the pains of exile to the pleasures of home, earned with the wages of corruption. Lucas, I believe, has had no biographer, therefore such remarks of him as I am able to give from pamphlets and magazines will be of interest and appropriate, filling in the traits and transactions of the Irish Parliaments.

The county of Clare claims the honour of his nativity. His father in the early years of the eighteenth century held a farm under the Earl of Carrick, and in this farm-house, in the year 1713, Charles Lucas first saw the light of day. He did not live long among the pleasant fields, the round towers, the verdant banks of the Shannon or Fergus. His father was not a provident farmer, and sold whatever interest he possessed in his land, removing with his family to Dublin, where Charles Lucas enjoyed the advantage of a classical education, and obtained his degree in the Dublin University. His taste was for the healing art, and he became an apothecary. When admitted to practise, he opened a shop for the sale of medicine on the banks of the Liffey—Ormond Quay.

He was not devoid of literary as well as political ambition, but his first essay in print had reference to his profession. In 1735, when about the age of twenty-two, he published a pamphlet which awakened the wrath of the Dublin apothecaries. It was entitled " A Scheme to prevent Frauds and Abuses in Pharmacy ;" and he sought the intervention of the Irish Legislature to protect the people of Ireland in general, and the inhabitants of Dublin in particular, from the danger of using drugs of so inferior a description that they could not be used elsewhere. It was asserted that, on some English vendors of drugs being accused of selling unsound and dangerous drugs, likely to prove hurtful to the natives of Great Britain, the defence was, there was no danger to their fellow-subjects in England or Scotland, as they sent all such drugs to Ireland. The exposure of this state of the medicine chest alarmed the Legislature, and caused the passing of an Act, subjecting the apothecaries' shops in Dublin to be visited and examined, same as those in London. Yet this praiseworthy attempt to remedy so glaring a mischief, instead of gaining for the author the thanks of the Dublin apothecaries, had the very opposite result ; and he tells us " he fell under the universal rage of his brethren, who combined against him, and stirred up enemies against him, among the two other branches of the profession." He seems to have had a good deal of humour as well as satire in his disposition. In a pamphlet bearing the singular title of "Pharmacomastrix," he gives a comic, yet natural description of a doctor visiting a patient. It is evidently an attempt to pay off some of the annoyances he sustained from the Dublin faculty. "Assuming a pedantic air, one of these gentlemen examines the tongue, and feels the pulse of the patient, with great solemnity; then in a long-spun jargon of technical phrases (enough to excite the surprise of half the nurses in Christendom), he asks a set of unintelligible questions. When the poor patient makes an attempt to answer, the wily quack, with mighty revolving 'humph'—'I thought so' —'I apprehend' sounds, with fatal pen and ink prescribes largely some pernicious burning spirit, which he calls Alexipharmic, not knowing but he is signing the sufferer's death-warrant, though he meant only to draw a small bill in his own favour."

Through the useful agitation which Lucas kept up against the importation of adulterated drugs into Ireland, the Act passed to prevent their sale with impunity, which was first only for a limited period, but was renewed. Emboldened by his success in reforming the Dublin apothecaries, Lucas next applied his energies to effecting a reform in the Dublin corporation. The Board of Aldermen had long asserted and enjoyed a monopoly in power and the lucrative appointments. The Commons naturally chafed at this. By the Irish Corporate Charters, the election of mayors and other officials was vested in the citizens. In 1662 the Irish Parliament by statute empowered the lord-lieutenant to make rules for the Irish corporations, and by these rules the aldermen, who were very much under Government control, ruled the corporations in the Irish boroughs. In 1741 Lucas was elected a town councillor of Dublin, and, assisted by another member of the common council, James Digges Latouche, a member of the respectable Huguenot family of that name, a family always identified with civil and religious liberty, set about examining the privileges of the aldermen. He discovered that the new rules did not give them power of electing members of their Board. The right of such appointments being insisted upon by the aldermen, the question as to the legality was brought in the form of a *Quo Warranto* against the junior alderman in the Court of King's Bench.

The judges then were Chief Justice Morlay, with Judges Wood and Rose. The judges were then dependent upon the Crown, and seldom dared to act save according to the will of the prime minister. The case was argued for four days, and the decision of the Court was in favour of the alderman. Lucas published a pamphlet, commenting on the decision, which he attributed to the slavish condition of the judges. This production was printed under the name of "Complaints of Dublin." Lucas presented two copies of the brochure to the then viceroy, Lord Harrington, who did not vouchsafe to notice it. As the king's lieutenant did not appear to notice this production, Lucas resolved to see what could be done by placing the matter before the supreme ruler of the empire. He translated the Charter of Dublin from the Latin, and dedicated the translation to King George II. As the viceroy was in England, lords justices ruled Ireland in his stead, and to these Lucas sent copies of the charter, with one designed for his Majesty. But the lords justices felt that a production which set forth that the citizens had been robbed of their corporate rights by the aldermen—and failing to obtain justice for his fellow-citizens in Ireland, Lucas appealed to the throne—was little short of a censure upon the Irish executive, they politely acknowledged the receipt of the work, which they declined to send to the king. A contest for the representation of the Irish metropolis was the next occasion on which Lucas displayed his zeal for the citizens. Sir James Somerville, who represented the city, died in 1748. Lucas's associate in the town council, Mr. James Digges Latouche, started as the popular candidate, and was opposed by Sir Samuel Cooke, whose pretensions were supported by the weight of the aldermen. The people were resolved to oppose the nominee of the aldermen, and this resolve probably induced Lucas to offer himself as a candidate, for, as Latouche was already in the field, we should have thought Lucas was thus dividing the popular support and giving Cooke a better chance of success. Fortunately, however, for the popular cause, the death of the second member for Dublin City, Alderman Pearson, prevented any rivalry between Latouche and Lucas. The popular party had now the opportunity of electing two advocates of Irish freedom. The aldermen were not inclined to give a chance to the candidates of the Liberals. They put Mr. Charles Barton, who had filled the office of high sheriff in 1733, in nomination. This contest created much excitement. The rival candidates delivered stirring addresses in the public halls. The reception afforded by the people to Lucas and Latouche was so enthusiastic, and their opponents received so badly, they soon left the popular favourites in undisputed possession of the platform. They worked, however, most actively in private. Pending the election, the Irish Government made a determined effort to deprive the country of the services of Lucas. He published twenty "Addresses to the Citizens of Dublin." These Addresses breathed forth a spirit of patriotism that was only second to that which Swift printed in the Drapier's Letters. In his denunciation of popular tumult, Lucas seems to have anticipated O'Connell, who, when warning the people against breaking the peace, said, "Whoever commits a crime gives strength to the enemy." Lucas declared, "My cause is the cause of order; he who commits a breach of the peace is the enemy of Lucas and liberty." In a series of pamphlets called the "Censor," he lashed the enemies of the people. Lucas lost no time when his Excellency returned to Dublin in presenting him with copies of his "Addresses." The viceroy tried blandishments, treated Lucas with extreme civility, and so won upon his opinion, that Lucas praised him; but not altering his views, to suit the Castle party, in the usual speech from the throne at the opening of Parliament, the lord-lieutenant strongly recommended the Legislature to examine and punish all attempts to "spread disaffection and discontent." The publications of Lucas were scrutinised, and sedition said to be extracted. He and his printer were called to the bar of the House of Commons. The copy of the Addresses which Lucas had presented to the viceroy supplied the evidence upon which, on the 16th October 1749, the Irish House of Commons declared that "Charles Lucas was an enemy to his country."

This disgraceful decision was near creating a commotion in the metropolis. Lucas was addressing a meeting of the citizens in reference to some municipal reforms at the Tholsel, when the serjeant-at-arms came to arrest him. When informed of this, he paused in his speech, and said, "My friends, I have been prepared for this. I grieve, indeed, that my country's liberty should be wounded, but I feel too much honour in being the victim of her enemies." He then continued with great coolness the address which was interrupted, and having exhausted the subject, prepared to accompany the officer of the law. The people sought to restrain him, and volunteered to defend him from any attempt at arrest. "We are here in thousands," they said, "and we are your friends." He replied, "No; let me suffer, but let not one drop of blood be shed." Some little time was allowed for him to prepare for his imprisonment. He returned to his own house, and wrote to the governor of the gaol of Newgate, asking for the indulgence of a fire in a private room, as he was in very inferior health. This slight favour was denied. Lucas was informed that the governor's orders were that he should be confined in the common room, having only a bed of straw to lie upon, and criminals for companions. This information, aided by the expostulations of his friends, who urged him to fly, induced him to forego his intentions of braving the worst, and abiding the order of the House of Commons. He was conveyed to the sea-shore, where a boat was in waiting, by means of which he reached the Isle of Man. From thence he passed to Westminster; and this treatment of a citizen for endeavouring to serve his fellow-men was thus rebuked by the great English moralist, Samuel Johnson: "The Irish ministers forced him from his native country, by methods equally irresistible by guilt and innocence; let the man thus driven into exile for having been the friend of his country be received in every other place as a confessor of liberty, and let the tools of power be taught that they may rob but cannot impoverish."[1]

"This language," as has been remarked by a competent critic, "reflects honour on the writer and the subject."[2] The electors of Dublin, when

[1] Boswell, vol. ii. p. 259.
[2] James Burke in his sketch of Lucas in *Duffy's Fireside Magazine*, April 1852.

deprived of the opportunity of returning Lucas, started Mr. Thomas Reid, a merchant, in his stead, but Latouche was the more successful of the two popular candidates. He was returned as the colleague of Sir Samuel Cooke, though the aldermen, aided by the Castle party, strove hard to keep him out, and elect Mr. Barton in his room. A petition against Mr. Latouche's return was presented by Mr. Barton, and referred to á committee. His alleged disqualification was the countenance and support he displayed in regard to Lucas, and this, it was urged, rendered him unfit to be a member of the Irish House of Commons. The argument was deemed sufficient to unseat him, and the petitioner, who was next on the poll, declared duly elected.

The course pursued towards the banished Lucas was published in a pamphlet, entitled "A Critical Review of the Liberty of the British Subject, with a View to the Proceedings of the House of Commons in Ireland, against an unfortunate Exile of that Country, who, contending for the Rights and Liberties of the Public, lost his own." This production was powerfully written, and the authorship was attributed to Lucas himself. A reply was printed—the production of Sir Richard Cox. He had previously written against Lucas under the *nom de plume* of Anthony Litton, a Cork surgeon. This production of Cox called forth a crushing answer from the critical reviewer, which closed the controversy. Lucas did not allow his pen to rust while he was in London. In his safe retreat in

Westminster, he levelled his arrows of sarcasm across the Irish Sea, and published "A Denunciation of Tyrannic Governors as a Caution to London." He seems to have studied the interests of the London corporation as well as that of the Irish metropolis, for he published "A Letter to the Free Citizens of London," which he expected the lord mayor would present to the corporation, and requested him to do so, but his request was not complied with. Probably not finding an avenue for his desire to spread the feelings of liberty with which he was stirred in England, he went abroad, and took the degree of M.D. at Leyden. On his return to London he delivered scientific lectures, and devoted himself to the practice of his profession. In 1756 he published an *Essay on Water*, which obtained him much repute. At this period of literary history dedications to opulent or eminent patrons was a frequent practice, and Lucas was not above adopting this general though often servile course. He published his Water Essay in three volumes. The first he dedicated to Prince George, shortly known in British history as King George III. The second volume was dedicated to Lord Anson, the circumnavigator; and the last to Lord Shelburne, who, judging from the terms in which Lucas writes of him, was the fittest to receive a compliment at his hands. Of this excellent nobleman Lucas says: "In my prosperity I was honoured by your friendship in Ireland. In that, however, there was nothing strange; the prosperous never want worldly friends. But, my lord, you stood the test of adversity; for, when oppression stripped me of the rights of a freeborn subject, and reduced me to exile, my distresses were mitigated by the thought that I still had your friendship, and that of men like you. *That* supported my drooping spirits in my exile, and taught me to smile amidst adversity. Must I not acknowledge my gratitude! I must; and rather than be unmindful of your kindness, may my right hand forget its cunning."[1]

The *Essay on Water* gained the author much favourable notice from scientific bodies. It analysed the component substances of which water is formed, and the various mineral springs of Great Britain and the Spas of Germany—in fact, to some extent anticipating Dr. Granville's work.

In 1760, his friends having caused the attorney-general to enter a *nolle prosequi* on the indictment against him, he was induced to return to his native land. The death of King George II. and accession of his grandson, George III., caused the dissolution of the old, and the election of a new Parliament. Lucas was hailed on his return with the acclamation due to his services and his sufferings. He was offered the representation of Dublin, and, on consenting to become a candidate, a committee was formed which secured his triumphant return. He became a very active and useful member. One of the evils which afflicted the political system of Ireland in his time was the duration of Parliament.

[1] *Essay on Water*, vol. iii.

The members being elected for the life of the sovereign, were to a great extent irresponsible, and could represent or misrepresent their constituents as their conscience dictated. It was not so in England. There the duration of Parliament being limited to seven years, gave the electors a hold upon the conduct of the members, who could not hope for re-election if they neglected or abused their duties as members of the House of Commons. Lucas felt this a legitimate opportunity for effecting reformation. In 1763 he brought before the House the heads of a Bill to bring about the practice in England, and limit the duration of the Parliament to six years. He obtained support from the patriot band then growing in power and strength. It was the first time the celebrated Henry Flood gave indications of that fervid oratory which afterwards made him the rival of Grattan in eloquence. The measure was sent to England, according to the requirements of Poynings' Law, and there altered from a sexennial to octennial, it is said in the expectation of being rejected in Ireland; but if so the expectation was not founded on a knowledge of the Irish Parliament. The change was not regarded as of sufficient importance to cause the rejection of the amended Bill, so the Octennial Act was passed. This was a step in the right direction, and gave Lucas a basis to work upon. He advocated other measures of reform, and applied himself vigorously to stem the tide of corruption which was the mode by which the Government defeated the advocates of liberty in the House,

He was of infirm health, and, like that accomplished gentleman who sat recently in the House of Commons, Mr. Kavanagh, had to be carried in and out of the House. Here his countenance, strikingly handsome, derived added interest from his silvery locks. He was remarkable for the care and neatness of his attire, and no stranger ever entered the House without being struck by his appearance and inquiring his name.[1]

In 1763 Lucas started the *Freeman's Journal*, a newspaper which, after more than a century, flourishes at the present day. The columns of this popular journal at the period of its young existence were enriched by the contributions of men whose names are household words among those who love the name of Ireland — Lucas, Grattan, Flood, Hussey Burgh, Barry Yelverton, afterwards Lord Avonmore. To Lucas there may be ascribed the establishment of the newspaper press of Ireland as the advocate and supporter of the cause of Irish nationality.

While in Parliament Lucas asserted the right of the Irish Parliament to legislate for Ireland. He argued that, as Ireland was a kingdom, her king, Lords, and Commons alone had right to make the laws for the Irish people. He also tried to control the number of places and pensions which the Government gave as rewards for the support they received in order to carry their financial measures in defiance of the popular opposition.

[1] Hardy's *Life of Lord Charlemont*.

It must have been a source of great satisfaction to the Irish patriot, that the independence of Ireland was assured ere he died. Just as the dawn of Irish freedom was breaking through the clouds which so long had engulfed it, Dr. Lucas died. A brief but most deserved complimentary notice of his death appeared in the *Freeman's Journal*, and amidst the universal regret of all lovers of that liberty to which he devoted his talents and the labours of his active life, Dr. Lucas was consigned to an honoured grave in St. Mechan's Church, Dublin.

CHAPTER XIV.

1767–1791.

Henry Flood, born in 1740—Member for Kilkenny—Equals Lucas in most eminent Parliamentary Talents—Accepts Office—Anger of the People—Character of the Government—Attacks on Flood by Scott—Attorney-General's comical Description of Flood under the name of Harry Plantagenet—Dispute with Grattan—Enters the British Parliament—Return to Ireland—Death in 1791—Made a large Bequest to Trinity College, Dublin—Grattan's post-mortem Eulogy.

ONE of the most effective allies of Dr. Lucas, in his efforts to reform the Irish Parliament, was Henry Flood. He ably supported the doctor in limiting the duration of Parliament from the longevity of a sovereign's life, which we know, in the case of George III., was sixty years, and we pray in the case of Queen Victoria may be longer.

Henry Flood, born about 1740, was son of Chief Justice Warden Flood. His career in college was marked more by dissipation than literary faculty; but he soon grew weary of the orgies then so freely indulged in by the fast youth of the Irish metropolis, and he resolved, by severe toil, to make amends for hours of folly. He soon entered Parliament as member for Kilkenny, and became one of the leaders of the Opposition. He attacked the satellites of the Government with undaunted courage and unrivalled power. He was regarded as equal to Grattan in patriotism, and his superior in statesmanship; and that great Irishman has left us the following estimate of his contemporary:—" Mr. Flood, my rival as he is called, and I should be unworthy the character of his rival, if, in his grave, I did not do him justice. He had his faults, but he had great powers, great public effect. He persuaded the old, he inspired the young; the castle vanished before him. On a small subject he was miserable; put into his hand a distaff, and, like Hercules, he made sad work of it; but give him a thunderbolt, and he had the arm of a Jupiter. He misjudged when he transferred himself to the English Parliament. He forgot that he was a tree of the forest, too old and too great to be transplanted at fifty; and his seat in the British Parliament is a caution to the friends of union to stay at home and make the country of their birth the seat of their action."

On entering Parliament, he immediately became the ally of Mr. Lucas in opposing the Government. He took part in all the great debates in the Irish House of Commons in support of measures brought forward for the benefit of Ireland. In 1767, the Octennial Act, limiting the existence of Parliament to eight years, was passed. Previously the Parliament generally was not dissolved during the life of the sovereign. The right of the Irish House of Commons to vote money bills framed by themselves was asserted by refusing a Bill sent from the English Parliament. This spirit of independence provoked the anger of the British Government, and the viceroy, Lord Townshend, prorogued the Irish Parliament to the year 1771. At the meeting of the House of Commons, an Act was passed which permitted Roman Catholics, who formerly were not allowed to hold lands, to take bogs, on the conditions of reclaiming half the holdings within twenty-one years, and on failure of this condition the lands were to be forfeited. In 1775 the American revolt took place, and during the continuation of this struggle the Irish House of Commons revoked many of the enactments of the Penal Code, which so grievously oppressed the Catholics.

The fact that Flood, the pupil and associate of Lucas, and the able associate of Grattan, having accepted office, caused so complete a revulsion in the populace that must have pained him deeply. From being the idol of the people, he was so hooted in the streets that the protection of a guard was suggested; and if the language of Scott, the attorney-general, in the course of an attack in the House was true, he actually had the protection of a guard. As on another occasion Scott gave a faithful account of his rise and fall in popularity under the assumed name of Harry Plantagenet, I introduce it here as a trait showing the style of debate sometimes permitted in the Irish Parliament.

At this time the character of the Government of Ireland was not high in public esteem. Even the actions of Mr. Flood and his ability exerted in the cause of Ireland did not avert the shafts of satire. In a poetic account of the dispensing of ministerial patronage we find them thus described :—

> "They nibbled away both night and day,
> Like mice in a round of Glos'ter ;
> They're big rogues all, both great and small,
> From Flood to Leslie Foster."

One of the dispensers of Government gifts being asked why the Phœnix Park, then flooded by surface water, since easily removed, was not drained, replied, "Faith, we're too busy draining the rest of Ireland."

When he left office, he was of course open to attacks from the Castle party. Scott thus refers to him :—"The right hon. gentleman has the happy talent of turning everything to his advantage. When he became an object of popular resentment, he traversed the streets with a guard. He looked melancholy at the bar, sighed in the House, cried in the council, and blubbered in the ante-chamber. The people were astonished, the women went into mourning, Government thought all her functions were suspended, and nothing could allay the general concern but a plentiful reversion for the most noble gentleman. When the fleets of England, at a great expense, made a number of little descents on the French coast last war, it was wittily said, 'We were breaking panes of glass with guineas ;' and though his house is filled with most elegant furniture, I will venture to say that no part of it cost as much as the *crown glass* with which his windows were repaired."

A curious mode of discussing an important subject is related in the *Irish Parliamentary Register*, vol. i. p. 125. Mr. Bushe brought forward the Mutiny Bill, which Mr. Grattan seconded. Mr. Flood taking part in the debate, roused the criticism of Mr. Scott, attorney-general, afterwards Chief Justice Lord Clonmel. "There is not," he said, "any reason for the honourable gentleman's frequent mention of corruption. If a rebellion could be raised, no man possesses more ability to promote it; if stopped, no man possesses greater ability to allay it. Thus powerful as he is, I hope he will consider the people, and that his wrath may not be like that of Achilles, only to be appeased by the blood of his country. I perceive, Mr. Speaker, that we are all growing warm, and if the House will permit me, I will tell you a story, which may help to bring us to better temper. When I was at the Temple, there was a parish clerk that used to raise the psalm, and who went by the name of *Harry Plantagenet*. I had taken it into my head the family of the Plantagenets was quite extinct, and was induced by curiosity to ask this man how he came to be called by that name. Accordingly I went to him one day, and mentioned my wish to know his story. 'I was once a king, sir,' said he, 'and reigned with uncontrolled dominion over hound and greyhound, bugle and horn, by which I have acquired this name; but if you please, I will relate my story at large.' 'Go on, Harry,' said I. 'I lived in the neighbourhood of Windsor Forest when a boy, and used frequently to divert myself with hunting the king's deer, for I always loved to hunt the *king's* deer.' '*Go on, Harry,*' *said I.* 'I hallooed and I shouted so loud often that there was not a dog of the pack but what obeyed my voice, not a lad in the forest but attended my call.' 'Go on, Harry,' said I. 'At last, sir, the chief huntsman, perceiving what command I had over the dogs, the sportsman resolved to take me into his pay.' '*Go on,*' *said I.* 'I accepted of his offer; but I now found myself so much at my ease, that I grew indolent, and insisted on riding out to hunt in *furniture,* for I always loved to hunt in furniture.' 'Go on, Harry,' said I. 'I was indulged with furniture; but I soon perceived that the younger fellows, who could now outride me, became greater favourites with the chief huntsman.' 'Go on, Harry,' said I. 'This stung me to the quick, and I determined to pick a quarrel. Some of the fringe of my furniture, which was torn, and which I would have repaired at the chief huntsman's expense.' '*Go on, Harry.*' 'I immediately began to hunt in opposition, but not a dog obeyed my hollo or sportsman attended my call.' '*Go on, Harry.*' 'I hallooed as I went until I was weary, but still without any effect. I had the mortification to find that I had totally lost my influence in the forest, and I retired to this parish to devote the rest of my days to the making of my soul, and I now raise the psalm and join in the thanksgiving.' This, sir, is the story of *Harry Plantagenet*, and this story I would apply to every man who cannot be quiet without expense, or angry without rebellion."

On the attorney-general sitting down, Mr. Flood rose. He said: "I am unable to perceive the smallest similitude between this story and my situation, except that my name is *Harry*. I have indeed been a huntsman, but then I was never whipper-in."

The resolutions passed at the convention must ever entitle the descendants of the Ulster volunteers of Dungannon to the gratitude of their Roman Catholic fellow-countrymen, were promoted by Mr. Flood. He is thus described by the Right Hon. J. T. Ball: "Possessed of extensive knowledge on political subjects (the fruit of much study and reflection), speaking with force and clearness, an acute thinker and an accurate reasoner, he, more than any other leader of his time, contributed to elevate the tone of discussion in the House of Commons. It was by his example that the members were first guided to the excellence in debate which they afterwards attained. It is no wonder the Irish Government desired to procure the services of so valuable an ally in the rapidly spreading desire to remove the disabilities under which Ireland laboured, and, feeling desirous of enabling remedial measures to be brought forward, Mr. Flood accepted office."[1]

Though, while Grattan and Flood were bravely advancing the cause of Irish independence, some occasional differences of opinion elicited angry words between them, which caused great sorrow to the friends of both statesmen, it was an unfortunate event that disagreement arose through the Act of 6 George I. Though the independence of Ireland was declared in 1782, and Grattan considered this gave a full and complete surrender of British legislature and judicial supremacy over Ireland, Flood considered the surrender was not fully stated, and required a more precise enactment, which was passed; but the discussion caused the two great orators to use language towards each other which, following the patriotic and Christian example of the late Mr. MacCarthy, I omit to quote.[2] Also Mr. Flood was willing to have some demonstration of the volunteers in his efforts to bring about a reform in the House of Commons, and this Grattan strenuously and successfully resisted.

Feeling perhaps some hostility to Grattan, Mr. Flood resolved to change the scene of his senatorial talents, and bought for £4000 a seat in the British House of Commons. Here, however, his peculiar style of reasoning did not meet with the success expected, and, as Grattan observed, he was too old to be transplanted. It is thought he was not

[1] *Historical Review.*
[2] *Life of Grattan,* p. 47.

treated well by the Duke of Buckingham, who at the next election took away the seat from Mr. Flood. He had a considerable fortune, which he bequeathed to Trinity College, Dublin, and died at his seat in County Kilkenny, in 1791, sincerely regretted.

CHAPTER XV.

HENRY GRATTAN. BORN 1746; DIED 1820.

Born in 1746—Recorder Grattan opposed to his Son's Politics—Is disinherited—A Law Student—Encounter in Windsor Forest—Called to the Irish Bar in 1772—Member for Charlemont in 1775—Efforts for Free Trade—English Hostility to Irish Industries—By Aid of the Volunteers Irish Independence gained—Political Changes in England—Viceroys changed in Ireland—Fox's Manœuvring—Great Excitement in Dublin in April 1782—Grattan in the Front—He obtains Ireland's Freedom—Vote of £100,000 to Grattan—Accepts Half—The State of Ireland in 1798 causes him to abandon attending Parliament—The Debate on the Union—Grattan's last Appeal—The Union Act—Grattan returns to Tinnahinch—Elected to represent Dublin in the United Parliament—His Fame as an Orator—The Champion of the Roman Catholics—Death—Last Words.

THE career of this great Protestant patriot has been so frequently written, I would not feel justified in attempting to add to the number. I shall content myself with some particulars of his birth, education, and career. Henry Grattan was born in Dublin in 1746. His father was recorder of Dublin, and had for his colleague in the representation of the Irish metropolis Mr. Lucas. But they were of decidedly adverse politics. While Lucas, as I have shown, was an ardent Nationalist, devoting all his energies to the independence of Ireland, Recorder Grattan opposed this spirit; and, finding his son Henry espoused the views, and no doubt was early educated in them, of Dr. Lucas, did all he could to induce his son to abandon them. Finding Henry was immovable, the angry recorder marked his sense of the son's opposition to his political sentiments by depriving him of the paternal property, and leaving him dependent on a small income derived from his mother.

Henry Grattan became a law student, and during his terms in London, tired of the confinement of the city, he took lodgings in Windsor, and was accustomed to take nocturnal rambles in Windsor Forest. He seems at this time to be practising that talent in which he afterwards displayed such consummate ability—public speaking, and caused his landlady to have some suspicion of his sanity, as she often heard him shouting in his room, and calling on one Mr. Speaker, though she knew no one else was present. An anecdote is related of his midnight orations. While in the glades of Windsor he beheld a gibbet, where some malefactor had been hung, but the cord dangled unoccupied. This afforded a meet theme for the young orator, who was vehemently addressing the vacant gibbet, when he was touched on the shoulder by some other nightly rambler, who pointed to the empty place of punishment, and inquired, "How the mischief did you get down?"

Grattan's reply was prompt.

"Sir," said he, "I perceive you have an interest in asking that question."

Grattan was called to the Irish Bar in 1772, and went the Home Circuit, where he had some practice. He soon gave up the legal profession, for which we can readily believe he was not suited. It is said he used to return his fees when the cases in which he was retained were decided against his clients. Another pursuit, more congenial to his taste, and better suited to his talents, was henceforth to claim him. The brother of the Earl of Charlemont, Major Coalfield, who was member for the family borough of Charlemont, was drowned in 1775, and the earl bestowed the seat on the talented Henry Grattan.

In that admirable *Historical Study of Grattan* by Mr. John George MacCarthy, the young men of Ireland may learn the claims Henry Grattan has to be enshrined in the Irish heart. Here, in choice and elegant as well as eloquent words, the late talented Mr. J. G. MacCarthy traces the career of this great Irish patriot. We learn from this able work his early culture, from his birth in 1746 to the period of his taking his seat for the borough of Charlemont in 1775. His noble struggles to remove the barriers to the commercial freedom of Ireland, which English jealousy and cupidity had imposed, are fully told. The restrictions on trade having been removed, Grattan determined to induce the Irish Parliament to assert its independence. Many opposed his views, alleging that sufficient had been gained, and a resolution was passed by the House of Lords, on a motion by the Duke of Leinster, that the agitations of misguided men should be discouraged, as it diverted the people from prospering by commercial advantage.

But neither Lords nor Commons could divert Grattan from his course. On the 19th April 1780 he proposed, "That the king's most excellent Majesty and the Lords and Commons of Ireland are the only powers competent to make laws to bind Ireland."[1]

Though these enactments were so far yielding independence to the Irish Parliament, another Act had to be passed repealing Poynings' Law. This was done by statute 21 & 22 Geo. III. c. 47, and a mode directed for the future legislation in Ireland.[2]

Mr. Corry, the Chancellor of the Exchequer, having taunted Grattan with raising the rebellion in 1798, had reason to repent of his charge, and was thus replied to:—

"Has the gentleman done—has he completely done? He was unparliamentary from the beginning to the end of his speech. There was scarcely a word he uttered that was not a violation of the privileges of the House, but I did not call him to order. Why? Because the limited talent of some

---

[1] *Grattan's Life*, by his Son, vol. ii.
[2] For summary of the speech, see *Hist. Review*.

men render it impossible for them to be severe without being unparliamentary. But before I sit down I shall show him how to be severe and parliamentary at the same time. On any other occasion I should think myself justifiable in treating with silent contempt anything that might fall from that honourable member; but there are times when the insignificance of the accuser is lost in the magnitude of the accusation. I know the difficulty the honourable member laboured under when he attacked me. Conscious that, on a comparative view of our characters, public and private, there is nothing he could say which would injure me. The public would not believe the charge. I despise the falsehood. If such a charge was made by an honest man, I would answer it in the manner I shall do before I sit down. But I shall first reply to it when not made by an honest man, however, which I am proud to say was not greater than my deserts. I have returned to protect that constitution, of which I was the parent and the founder, from the assassination of such men as the honourable gentleman and his unworthy associates. They are corrupt, they are seditious, and they at this very moment are in a conspiracy against their country. I have returned to refute a libel, as false as it is malicious, given to the public under the appellation of a Report of a Committee of the Lords. Here I stand ready for impeachment or trial. I dare accusation. I defy the honourable gentleman. I defy the Government; I defy their whole phalanx. Let them come forth. I tell the ministers I will neither give them quarter nor take it. I am here to lay the statement. The right honourable gentleman says, 'I fled from the country after exciting rebellion, and that I had returned to raise another.' No such thing. The charge is false. The civil war had not commenced when I left the kingdom, and I would not have returned without taking a part. On the one side, there was the camp of the rebel; on the other, the camp of the minister, a greater traitor than the rebel. The stronghold of the constitution was nowhere to be found. I agree that the rebel who rises against the Government should have suffered, but I miss on the scaffold the right honourable gentleman. Two desperate parties were in arms against the constitution. The right honourable gentleman belongs to one of those parties, and deserves death. I could not join the rebels. I could not join the Government. I could not give torture. I could not give half-hanging. I could not give free quarters. I could take part with neither. I was therefore absent from the scene when I could not be active without self-reproach, nor indifferent to safety. Many honourable gentlemen thought differently from me. I respect their opinion, but I keep my own; and I think now, as I thought then, that the treason of the ministers against the liberties of the people was infinitely worse than the rebellion of the people against the ministers. I have returned, not as the right honourable member has said, to raise another storm. I have returned to discharge an honourable debt of gratitude to my country, that confers a great reward for past services, I hope not undeserved.

"It is not a little singular that the city of Cork, which has shown such vigour in seeking the repeal of the Union, should have been the principal strength of the Government in its support of this measure. Under date of 23rd April 1800, I find, at a meeting of the City Grand Jury, held during the Spring Assizes in the city, in the Grand Jury room, it was resolved unanimously that the sentiment of the city of Cork in favour of a legislative union with Great Britain has already been expressed in the most decided and unequivocal manner, and that the ineffectual efforts which have been made to represent this city as entertaining a contrary opinion, affords the most decisive evidence that the great majority of our fellow-citizens, in point of wealth, loyalty, and steady attachment to the constitution, still continue to approve of the measure."

This resolution was signed by the mayor, sheriffs, and common Speaker. But the unanimity was broken; for two most eminent citizens, Messrs. Purvis and Jeffrey, went as a deputation to present a petition to his Majesty, signed by leading merchants and freemen, in reprobation of the measure. Lord Cornwallis, however, was delighted at the apparent approval of Cork, while sternly contrasted with the hostility of Dublin. Writing to Mr.

Wickam, he says: "There is every reason to hope of a different sentiment." The efforts made by the viceroy to obtain what could be presented to Great Britain as showing the desire of the Irish nation to effect the union, are thus described by Mr. Plunket in the debate in the House of Commons, 15th January 1800: "During the whole interval between sessions, the barefaced system of Parliamentary corruption has been pursued—dismissals, promotions, threats, promises. In despite of all this, the minister found he could not succeed in Parliament, and so affected to appeal to what he had before despised, the sentiment of the people. Bribes were promised to the Catholic clergy; bribes were promised to the Presbyterian clergy. Though Grattan was prostrated by illness when the Bill for the Union was on for the third reading in the House of Commons, the entreaties of his family could not restrain him from once more urging the House to refuse assent to the measure. He felt the consequences of the measure being carried would inflict a deep blow upon the country he loved; so he left his sick-bed, and travelled from Tinnahinch to Dublin, a distance of about forty miles.

It is no wonder, when, wearied and fatigued by his journey, he appeared before the gaze of the members, cheer after cheer rang through the domed chamber, and his attached friends welcomed him warmly. His request that he would be allowed the indulgence of addressing the House from his seat, which the Speaker (Foster) readily yielded, he delivered one of the noblest pieces of parliamentary oratory ever heard in any assembly. The deep patriotism and pathos of its peroration could not be surpassed.

The last words of Grattan in the Irish Parliament are, I think, applicable now, as I think they amount to a prediction of a possible Home Rule Parliament in Ireland. "The constitution may for a time seem lost. The character of the country cannot be lost. The ministers of the Crown will find that it is not so easy to put down for ever an ancient and respectable nation by abilities, however great, and by power and corruption, however irresistible. Liberty may repair her golden beam, and with redoubled heat animate the country. The cry of loyalty will not be long continued against the principles of liberty. Loyalty is a noble, a judicious, and a capacious principle; but in these countries loyalty, distinct from liberty, is corruption, not loyalty. The cry of the connexion will not in the end avail against the principles of liberty. Connexion is a wise and a profound policy; but connexion without an Irish Parliament is connexion without its own principle; without analogy of condition, without the pride of honour which should attend it, is innovation, is peril, is subjugation — not connexion. The cry of disaffection will in the end avail against the principles of liberty. Identification is a solid and imperial maxim necessary for the preservation of freedom, necessary for that of empire; but without union of hearts, with a separate Government, and without a separate Parliament, identification is extinction, is dishonour, is conquest—not identification. Yet I do not give up my country. I see her in a swoon, but she is not dead. Though in her tomb she lies helpless and motionless, there is on her lips a spirit of life, and on her cheek a glow of beauty.

> 'Thou art not conquered, beauty's ensign yet
> Is crimson on thy lips and on thy cheek;
> And death's pale flag is not abroad there.'

"While a plank of the vessel holds together I will not leave her. Let the courtier present his loyal sail to the breeze, and carry the barque of his faith with every wind that blows: I will remain anchored here; with fidelity to the fortunes of my country, faithful to her freedom, faithful to her fall."

Had there been any general burst of antagonism in the country, had Catholics and Protestants and Presbyterians been of one national sentiment, such appeals as were made by Grattan, Plunket, Bushe, Curran, and Ponsonby would have effectually prevented the Bill from passing the Commons; but there was not. The Catholics were still the hewers of wood and drawers of water, unable to hold office or emolument in their native land, treated as unworthy to associate with their fellow-countrymen.

"The life of Grattan," says my gifted friend the late Daniel Owen Madden, "affords valuable lessons. It bids Irish Protestants not to entertain harsh prejudices against their Catholic fellow-countrymen, to look on all with a loving heart, to be tolerant of their infirmities caused by their unhappy history, and, like Grattan, earnestly to sympathise with all that is brave and generous in their character. It reminds the Irish Catholic that the brightest age of Ireland was when Grattan, a steady Protestant, raised it to proud eminence; that in the hour of his triumph he did not forget the state of the Catholics, but laboured through his virtuous life that all Catholics should enjoy unshackled liberty of conscience. He bids Irishmen of every creed to ponder upon the spirit and principles which governed the patriot's career in public and private."

It was very unfortunate that, on the question of Parliamentary Reform, Grattan should have opposed Flood. That statesman evidently distrusted the English ministers, and felt that, with the immense patronage of the proprietors of Irish boroughs, there was no safety if the measure of Union was proposed. The close of the last century, setting as it did in rebellion and disaster, left the country an easy prey to the wiles of Pitt, and so disheartened Grattan, he withdrew from Parliament, and left the Opposition of the Government to young, no doubt eloquent and patriotic members, notably Plunket, afterwards Lord Plunket, and Charles Kendal Bushe, afterwards Lord Chief Justice of the King's Bench. Against the Union they protested.

The career of Henry Grattan subsequent to the Union does not belong to this work. The Irish Parliament was no more. The independence of

Ireland was brief. As he pathetically said, "I watched over its cradle, and I followed its hearse." However, a few words must be added as to what was his career after the Irish Parliament ceased to sit in the noble building in College Green. He was a member of the Imperial Parliament, and devoted his great intellectual and oratorical powers to break the fetters which enchained his Catholic countrymen. Time after time he brought forward this Catholic Relief measure, doomed to be defeated, and, with the exception of a speech on the war with France in 1815, he rarely addressed the House of Commons save as the advocate of his country. The noble example of our Protestant patriots should induce our fellow-countrymen to hold out the hand of friendship. Then, Catholic fellow-Irishmen, remember the Christian advice of Father O'Leary:—"Let not religion, the sacred name of religion, which can in the case of an enemy discover a brother, be any longer a wall of separation to keep us asunder. We are all in some close degree allied, and it is time to forget past difference, and work harmoniously for the land of our birth."

After the Union Grattan retired to Tinnahinch, which was purchased with the money granted for his services in the cause of Ireland. Moore thus describes him:

> "Who that ever approached him when free from the crowd,
>   In a home full of love, he delighted to tread
> 'Mong the trees which a nation had given, and which bowed,
>   As if each brought a new civic crown to his head."

He greatly loved the pine-trees in his lawn, and when some one suggested the removal of one which interfered with a prospect from his house, he replied: "Oh no! if either is to come down, it must be the house, for it is the latest comer."

In 1805 he was elected member for Dublin, and went to the House of Commons at Westminster to advocate the claims of the Catholics to emancipation. They subscribed £4000 to defray the expenses of his election, but he declined to accept their liberality. On entering the House of Commons he sat down behind Fox, who said, "That is not the place for the Irish Demosthenes," and drew him to a seat beside himself. His fame as an orator brought many to the galleries of the House on the evening he was to address the House, and many feared, at his advanced age and peculiar style of speaking, he would not maintain his Irish reputation; but he did so fully, all the great speakers —Fox, Sheridan, Pitt— were enthusiastic in his praise. In 1819, though in delicate health, he retired to London, and though his family and friends endeavoured to dissuade him, and his physician warned him of the danger, like Parnell in later years, he persisted, and the country suffered the loss of his services. He died in London on the 6th June 1820, and was buried in Westminster Abbey, where Pitt, Fox, and other statesmen now rest.

When making a tour in the County Wicklow some years ago, I resolved to visit Grattan House of Tinnahinch. We were on our way to the Vale of Glendalough, and I bade our driver go to the country seat the nation gave to her patriot. We halted at the hall door, and I knocked. An aged female answered my summons, but to my request for admission she declined to permit my entrance. She said, " Lady Laura Grattan had given her orders that no stranger was to be allowed into the house in her absence." " Quite right of Lady Laura," I said ; " no stranger should enter this sacred house ; but I am no stranger. You may tell Lady Laura that no one can be a stranger acquainted with the life and glorious death of the immortal Grattan—that I am. I am sure you know how he went from this house, while dangerously sick, to make a last effort against the Union, and his pathetic words :

> 'Thou art not conquered, beauty's ensign yet
> Is on thy lips and on thy cheek,
> And death's pale flag is not abroad there.

Let the coaster present his flowing sail to the wind, and carry the light barque of his faith with every wind that blows : I will remain anchored here ; with fidelity to the fortunes of my country, faithful to her freedom, faithful to her fall.' "

I could see in the glistening eyes of the old lady that I had conquered. " Oh, sir," she said, " you indeed have a right to visit the house, you and your lady !" and as my wife accompanied me through the rather small but commodious hall, drawing-room, and parlour, we saw from the windows the clumps of well-grown trees—ash, oak, beech, and elm—which no doubt were the objects of Grattan's pride, which have outlived him, but with God's blessing may yet bloom and flower when another Grand Old Man restores an independent Parliament to Ireland.

CHAPTER XVI.

RIGHT HONOURABLE WALTER HUSSEY BURGH.
BORN 1743; DIED 1783.

Born in 1743—Education—Called to the Irish Bar, 1768—Letter on the Impolicy of Pledging Candidates—Joins the Opposition—While Prime Serjeant sacrifices Place for Patriotism—Specimens of his Oratory—Coincidence in Language between Hussey Burgh in 1769 and Lord George Bentinck in 1846—Appointed Chief Baron of the Exchequer in 1781—Death in 1783—Public Funeral—Pension on his Family—Praise by Grattan.

THIS distinguished patriot, statesman, and orator, of whom Ireland may feel justly proud, occupied a considerable place in Irish history during that brilliant period of her Parliament when it was enlightened by the genius and adorned by the eloquence of Flood and Grattan.

Walter Hussey Burgh, son of Ignatius Hussey, Esq. of Donore House, County Kildare, and Miss Elizabeth Burgh, was born in the year 1743. His original name was Walter Hussey, but he assumed the additional name of Burgh in pursuance of the will of a relative, who devised to him an estate in the county of Limerick, conditional on his taking the name of Burgh. Walter received his education at the school of Mr. Young in Abbey Street, and was prepared to enter the University of Dublin. He was an excellent classical scholar, and quite distinguished as a poet. Having selected the legal profession, and kept his terms, he was called to the Irish Bar in 1768. In those days, when owners of boroughs had the means of introducing young men of promise into Parliament, Walter Hussey had for this purpose the good offices of the Duke of Leinster; and in the year 1768 he was elected a member of the House of Commons. He soon was to make known his powers of oratory, but at first they showed more of the prodigality of a classical and poetic taste than was fitted for the deliberate assembly. This, however, was a fault in the right direction. Dr. Johnson truly says, it is easier to lop off redundancies than to supply deficiencies, and the fluency of young Hussey soon was regulated by the requirements of debate. He had tact and judgment to direct him, and very soon he was regarded as one of the most eloquent and powerful debaters in the Irish House of Commons.

Previous to the General Election in 1777, some questions of importance looming in the near future, many constituencies required from the candidates for their suffrage pledges that, when returned, their candidates were bound by their pledge to support or oppose the measures before the House in the way their constituents required. Among others seeking re-election was Hussey Burgh, and the views of so true a patriot and clear politician may be deemed serviceable on similar occasions. I am fortunate in having the means of stating them. They are addressed to an elector of Trinity College, Dublin, and I discovered the letter in the first volume of the *Anthologia Hibernica* :—

"DEAR HERBERT,—As I understand the business relating to a test, which was mentioned last night, is to be considered this afternoon in a large circle, and I am desirous that the same sentiments which I have already expressed to some of the independent electors may be known to all of them, I take the liberty of troubling you with the repetition of them, which, if you think proper, you will communicate. If the test required should be nothing more than a solemn engagement to act with integrity in the trust which you are about to respose in your candidates, there can be no other objection to it but the indelicacy of large professions, which in general are little else than the eulogium of one's own virtues. However, if it be any satisfaction to gentlemen who espouse this measure, I will and do give them the most solemn assurances that whileever I have the honour to sit in Parliament, I will, to the best of my judgment, pursue the real interest of this kingdom, without suffering any motives of profit or advancement to warp my sentiments or bias my vote. But at the same time that I make this declaration, I freely acknowledge that if gentlemen should have found no such promise in my conduct, they should pay but little attention to that of my pen. If by the test in contemplation it is proposed that your members should vote for or against any particular measure, I think it neither constitutional nor wise to enter into any previous promise by which deliberation shall be precluded; there is no seeing what new lights may be thrown on a subject, or what new circumstances may alter the merits of a question. If the member of an American Assembly had pledged his faith some years ago never to encourage a foreign trade in preference to that of the mother country, how different an aspect such a question would now wear from what could have been foreseen while the interests of Great Britain and her colonies were one. Am I then to say that I will steel my breast against conviction, and that I will regulate my conduct some years hence by the circumstances that now exist, without regard to what they may be at the time I am to act? Am I to go to the House of Commons liable to see changes and to hear arguments that may convince me that what I think advantageous may prove ruinous to the kingdom; and shall I expose myself to the dilemma of voting for ruin or breaking a solemn, perhaps the most solemn of promises? Is he an honest man who, with his eyes open, will run the hazard of such an alternative? If, again, the test is intended to restrain your member from taking any place, pension, or emolument under Government; as to a pension, I freely assure you I never will accept one, unless, perhaps, in this instance, if it should happen in the vicissitudes of affairs that I should grow old in an honourable employment,—I will suppose, for example's sake, on the Bench,—I shall think it no disgrace to accept a testimonial of having faithfully discharged my duties I should be no longer able to fulfil. This is so remote and improbable a contingency, that I should not mention it but for two reasons: the one, I intend these declarations to bend my whole life, I would suit them to every period of it; the other, that in disclaiming pensions in general I would avoid throwing an imputation on that just use of them whereby they are made the asylum of merit instead of the sanctuary of vice. I am an enemy to pensions, but the head that has long been watchful for the public welfare, let it at last find a pillow to repose upon; he who has long and laboriously cultivated the land, let him at last find a peaceful retreat beneath its honourable shade. Before I quit the article of pensions, I must observe to you that I consider an additional salary to a useless place on the same footing as a pension, only with these two differences: the one, that he who accepts what is in effect a pension, yet dares not own it by that name, plainly admits a consciousness of doing wrong; the other, that whereas the pension dies with the pensioner, the salary remains for ever. I think I need not further assure you I never will accept of such a salary. As to the test precluding your members from accepting an active employment, I confess it strikes me as highly exceptionable. Whatever is now determined by the College ought to set, and probably will set, an example to the whole kingdom. Do I set them to be universally determined that no man of independent principles shall have any share in the administration of government? While every other nation complains of the corruptions of her ministers, is Ireland going to resolve that she will have no minister but the most corrupt that can be found? Such a universal test will be a universal law that no man of public spirit shall be in office. Let us suppose for a moment that Nero had made such a law: 'Whereas the famed spirit of Roman patriotism has fallen into decay, be it therefore decreed that no man of integrity shall have any share in the conduct of public affairs.' Will you make a law that would have disgraced Nero? In what situation is it that a man can render best services to his country—where he can direct what is right, or where he is to oppose what is wrong; where he can preserve the fountain pure, or where he is to endeavour to purge the stream; where he can stifle mischief in its infancy, or where he must combat it if grown into a giant; where he can turn aside the uplifted shafts of power, or where he is to hold up his shield against them? But it will be said that experience tells us that men who come into office surrender their opinions at direction. Would to God there were more men who acted on real principle. The designing patriot will always become the corrupt courtier. If a man has no principle, he will make up in jobs what he denies himself in office; if he has principle, he will be honest at all times and in all situations. There are no slighter things than these paper kites which ride against the wind. But though I will not promise never to be in office, I will and do most solemnly promise never to be corrupt in office. When I see things ill-conducted, I will not promise not to conduct them better. But no emolument of office shall ever induce me to increase my expense. By not making emolument necessary to luxury, I will always be able to lay it down when it becomes inconsistent with my honour. In the armoury of virtue truth is the sword, and frugality the shield. Would any man wish that Lord Chatham had never been a minister? Had he taken such a test as is now thought of, England was undone. Should Lord Hardwicke and Lord Camden never have been chancellors? Every man's own recollection will furnish an hundred examples. You think the ship in danger; you complain of those at the helm; you tell me you have some dependence on my skill, or at least on my care, and what do you tell me? We will put you in the way of buffeting the man at the helm, but if you touch the rudder we will throw you overboard. One word more and I shall have done. Your endeavour is by some engagement to put it out of my power to desert the cause of truth. I will not conceal from you that I have some ambition. I would not anticipate the harvest of an honest reputation, and reduce every exertion of virtue to the bare right of performance of an exacted promise. I aspire to represent the College; 'tis not to be in Parliament, but to be thus in Parliament. 'Tis the honour of your confidence that I seek; I shall never court the brand of your distrust. —I remain yours, etc.,   W. H. BURGH."

This cogent reasoning prevailed, and he was duly elected for the Dublin University. One of his fellow-members gives the estimate of his character by stating, "He never allowed his own private interests to clash with his public duty."[1] When he held the dignified office of prime serjeant, in moving an amendment to an address from the throne, he said: "I never will support any Government in fraudulently concealing from the king the rights of his people. The high office which I possess can hold no competition with my principles and my conscience, and I shall consider the relinquishment of my gown as only a just sacrifice on the altar of my country. Strong statement rather than pathetic supplication is adapted to the crisis, and the amendment which I propose is, that it is not by expedients that this country is to be saved from impending ruin." Having resumed his seat, the consequences sure to follow from his thus assailing the executive government flashed upon his mind. He knew what the immediate result would be, and whispered to a friend who sat near, "I have now sealed the door against my own pre-

[1] *Curran and his Contemporaries*, p. 48.

ferment, and I have made the fortune of that man," indicating his successor, Mr. Brown.

The office which he thus relinquished is described by Sir Jonah Barrington:—" The office of prime serjeant, then the first law officer of Ireland, was filled at this period by one of the most amiable and eloquent men that ever appeared on the stage of politics, namely, Walter Hussey Burgh, whose conduct in a principal transaction rendered him justly celebrated and illustrious."

Sir Jonah Barrington thus sketches his character: —" Mild, moderate, and patriotic, Mr. Burgh was proud without arrogance, and dignified without effort; equally attentive to public concerns and careless of his own, he had neither avarice to acquire wealth, nor parsimony to retain it; liberal even to profusion, friendly to a fault, and disinterested to a weakness, he was honest without affluence, and ambitious without corruption; his eloquence was of the highest order—figurative, splendid, and convincing. The errors of his conduct were lost in the brightness of his virtues. At the Bar, the Parliament, and among the people, he was equally admired and universally respected."[1]

On all the great questions tending to establish the parliamentary independence of Ireland Mr. Burgh was a staunch advocate. When his friends regained office in 1781, he was restored to the place of prime serjeant. It is curious to find a parallel between a speech of his in 1769 and one

[1] *Annals of the Irish Parliament.*

of Lord George Bentinck in 1846. Describing the corrupt state of the Irish Parliament in 1769, Mr. Burgh said: "Our members are returned by the fear or dependence, not the affection or choice of the electoral body. Unaccountable for their conduct in Parliament, their venality is unrestrained, and universal corruption reigns in the House. They are the instruments of power—a set of men in regular pay, the janizaries of despotism."

During a debate on the Corn Laws in 1846, Lord George Bentinck said: "We are told by the Right Hon. Baronet that he would not consent to be a minister on sufferance; but I think he must be blinded indeed by the flattery of those around him, if he has not learnt that he is now a minister on sufferance, tossed from one side to the other, sometimes depending on the honourable gentlemen opposite, sometimes on friends around me, supported by none but his forty paid janizaries and some seventy other renegades, one-half of whom, while they support him, express their shame in doing so." [1]

Unfortunately we have no report of his speeches, but this eloquent passage has been preserved.

In about two years after this, in June 1783, he was appointed chief baron of the Court of Exchequer, on the death of Lord Tracton; but he did not live long to enjoy this dignity. He died on the 29th of September 1783, in the full vigour of his intellect, and fulness of his fame, at the early age of forty years. His fatal illness was said to have been contracted on

[1] *The Irish Bar*, p. 40.

circuit at Armagh, where the gaol fever prevailed. He left one son and four daughters, but no inheritor of his splendid talents. A public funeral was accorded to him, and his remains were followed to the grave by the members of the Legislature and the authorities and students of the University. After returning from his funeral, a grateful House of Commons conferred a pension of £2000 a year upon his five children, with benefit of survivorship.

Unfortunately of Hussey Burgh's splendid oratory few specimens remain. When preparing my late work, *The Irish Bar*, for publication, I tried in every direction to discover some of these magnificent orations with which he electrified the Irish House of Commons, and smote dismay into the hearts of Ireland's foes; but, alas! no Hansard existed in those days, and the Journals of the House only give the formal notices of daily routine. I am not the only author who was equally unsuccessful. In the valuable work of Mr. Phillips, called *Curran and his Contemporaries*, he says, in reference to Hussey Burgh: "I have heard but one sentence which has escaped unmutilated. Referring to the state of Ireland under English rule, and the embodiment of the National Army of 1782, the Irish Volunteers, Mr. Burgh warmed into this classical allusion, 'Talk not to me of peace. Ireland is not in a state of peace. It is smothered war. England has sown her laws like dragons' teeth, and they have sprung up armed men.'" I rejoice to say I have been more successful than Mr. Phillips, for, on reference to my

"Memoir of Hussey Burgh," in *The Irish Bar*, I find I discovered a longer specimen of his oratory than Mr. Phillips has given. It displays his utter disregard for self-interest — not a common quality in the Irish Bar in our times. On the motion of the Anglo-Irish Government to send 4000 Irish soldiers to uphold British rule in America during the War for Independence, Mr. Burgh refused his consent while taxation without representation was contended for. He closed his speech in these words: "Having no enemies to encounter, no partisans to serve, without passion, without fear, I have delivered my sentiments upon the present question—one of the greatest importance. I will not vote a single man against America without an accompanying address recommending conciliatory measures. I foresee the conclusion of this war. If ministers are victorious, it will be only establishing a right to the harvest after they have burned the grain—it will be establishing a right to the stream after they have cut off the fountain. Such is my opposition — a method ill calculated to secure emolument or to gain popularity. My conduct will not please either party. But I despise profit, I despise popularity, if the one is to be gained by base servility, and the other purchased by blind zeal. Farewell profit, farewell popularity, if, in acquiring you, fair fame is to be the victim."

Those who had the advantage of hearing his speeches place him above all his great contemporaries. Plunket said : " No modern speaker approached him in the power of stirring the passions;" and the Marquis Wellesley, another critical judge, ranked him superior to Pitt, Fox, or Burke.

CHAPTER XVII.

1792–1795.

Viceroyalty of Earl FitzWilliam—Administration of Earl FitzWilliam—Promise not to oppose the Catholic Relief Bill—In 1795, the Measure brought in by Gentleman John Beresford — Pitt complains of the Viceroy — Rumours that Lord FitzWilliam was to be recalled—Conduct of the British Government—Attempt to withhold Supplies—Lord FitzWilliam writes to Mr. Pitt—The popular Viceroy leaves Ireland — Grief for his Recall.

WHILE Mr. Pitt, no doubt, appeared desirous to remove the disabilities under which Catholics laboured—for though they were allowed to vote for the election of members, they were not allowed to sit in Parliament, and all offices of state, emoluments, and dignities were denied—there was no hope of redress from the Irish Parliament. In 1797, Grattan proposed a measure of relief in very moderate terms; but the spirit of animosity against the Catholics was so great, his measure was defeated by an overwhelming majority; the numbers being 19 for, 143 against.

On the 4th January 1790, the Marquis of

Buckingham was succeeded in the viceroyalty by the Earl of Westmoreland, and this nobleman's administration does not seem to have generally impressed the state of Irish politics. The Parliament seemed to vote the public money in a very scandalous way, and places and pensions were multiplied by Acts of Parliament.

The efforts to emancipate the Catholics were frustrated. A Convention Act, to prevent public meetings, was passed; and from some deep scheme of policy it would seem as if Mr. Pitt resolved, by selecting as viceroy a nobleman friendly to the Catholics, so to raise their hopes, and then, by suddenly withdrawing their friend, to incite the Irish people to try and gain by a rebellion he knew he had power to defeat, what they failed to obtain by constitutional means, and in the depressed state of Ireland accomplish his darling project of the Union.

The appointment of an assured friend gave great hopes to the Irish Catholics. On 4th January 1792, Lord FitzWilliam arrived in Ireland. He understood from Mr. Pitt he was to support the claims of the Catholics; and finding the law officers —Wolfe and Toler (afterwards Lord Norbury)— hostile to any recognition of the Catholic claim, gave their offices to friends of the people—Ponsonby and Curran. He seems to have had repeated interviews with Mr. Pitt, for the following extract from the *Freeman's Journal* gives a later date for his Irish visit:—

"In January 1795, Lord FitzWilliam arrived in Ireland, bearing a message of peace. He was welcomed, trusted by all creeds and classes. The old spirit of Protestant Ascendancy seemed to have departed, and a united Irish nation received with a *cead mille failthe* an English governor who had come to do justice to all. Great progress had been made in the Catholics question since 1793, when the Catholics were admitted to the elective franchise. All honour to the Protestant Episcopalians of Ireland. Though they had as a body at first stoutly resisted the extension of the franchise to the Catholics, yet when that measure was carried, practically, over their heads by the great organisation formed by Wolfe Tone and John Keogh, they bethought themselves of the whole case, and, encouraged by the presence of FitzWilliam and inspired by a sense of justice, they resolved to help in the work of Catholic emancipation.

"In July 1794, it was rumoured in Ireland that a Government favourable to the Catholic claims was about to be formed by the Duke of Portland and Mr. Pitt. The friends of the Catholics urged Grattan to proceed at once to England and see the new ministers. Grattan went. Arrived in London, he promptly called upon the Duke of Portland. 'I am glad to see you,' said the duke. 'I have taken office, and I have done so because I know that there is to be an entire change of system' (Grattan's *Memoirs*, vol. iv. p. 174). Shortly after this interview Grattan dined at the duke's with Pitt, the Grenvilles, George Ponsonby, Sir John Parnell, and others. Parnell and Pitt sat near each other at dinner. Pitt created an unfavourable impression both on Parnell and Grattan. They felt he was not to be trusted. 'What does Ireland want?' he said to Grattan—'what would she have more?' And this in 1794, when Irish Catholics had practically as little to do with the government of their country as the inhabitants of Mesopotamia.

"However, friendly relations were maintained between the Irish patriot and the English ministers. They saw each other frequently, and Grattan told Pitt frankly that the question of the hour was Catholic Emancipation. 'Ireland,' said Pitt, 'has already got much.' How like what Liberal Unionists say to-day! Finally, the terms arrived at between Grattan and Pitt were that the Government would not bring forward the Catholic question, but would not oppose it if some one else brought it forward. The exact words used by Pitt were 'not to bring forward the Catholic question.'

"Ponsonby, who sat on the ministerial bench, rose to his feet. He begged the subject might not be pressed further for the present, and that ministers should not be urged to answer Parsons' question. Grattan joined in the appeal, and the subject was allowed to drop. But on the 2nd of March Parsons returned to the topic again. When the report on supply was brought up, he moved that the words in the Money Bill, 'the 25th March 1796,' should be expunged, and the words, 'the 25th March 1795,' inserted instead. He denounced the conduct of the British Cabinet as disgraceful. 'There has been a meeting,' he said, 'held at the Royal Exchange. The governor of the Bank of Ireland was in the chair. Resolutions were passed, without a dissentient voice, in favour of the Catholics. The hopes of the people have been raised, and now in one instant they are to be blasted. The Protestants of Ireland have declared in favour of emancipation. But the British Cabinet cares neither for the Protestants nor the Catholics of Ireland. Has it come to this, that the British minister is to control all the interests, all the talents, all the inclinations of the people of this country?' Duquery followed in an equally violent speech. 'I have long watched,' he said, 'the British Cabinet, and I have ever discovered in it a strong propensity to treat Ireland with insult and contempt. I shall support my hon. friend (Parsons), for there is nothing like a Short Money Bill to bring the English minister to reason.' The chief secretary rose and begged Parsons to give way, Ponsonby and Grattan again joined in the appeal. It would not do, they said, in face of the troubles on the Continent, to vote a Short Money Bill. But Parsons and Duquery would not yield an inch. They wanted to know before they voted supplies for a twelvemonth, whether the British minister meant to keep his word or not.

"The House then divided, with the result—
    Against Parsons   . . 146
    For   24

"It was now officially announced that FitzWilliam was to be recalled. He had written to Pitt point-blank to say that he would not stand for one hour between the Catholics and emancipation, and Pitt informed him by next mail that he would be relieved from the government of the country.

"On the 25th of March Lord FitzWilliam left Ireland. 'It was,' says Plowden, 'a day of general gloom; the shops were shut; no business of any kind was transacted; and the whole city put on mourning. His coach was drawn to the water-side by some of the most respectable citizens, and a cordial sorrow was manifested, not only throughout Dublin, but the entire kingdom.'"

It appears that the good works of Lord Fitz-William were frustrated by the bigotry of the anti-Catholic party both in England and Ireland. Lord Clare was not to be denied, and he incessantly stirred up the embers of religious enmity against his fellow-countrymen.

On the 16th November 1792, Pitt wrote to Lord Westmoreland, then lord-lieutenant, his wish to promote the Union. He knew it was unpopular in Ireland. Lord Clare, the lord chancellor of Ireland, often pressed it on him. The attempt to bring the French Republicans to aid the party in Ulster, who so strongly identified themselves with the ferocious treaties of the French Republic, no doubt alarmed that sagacious statesman; and we learn from Mr. Fitzpatrick's recent contribution to Irish history, *Secret Service under Pitt*, how widespread was the conspiracy of the united Irish. These abominable plots were projected and matured chiefly in Ulster by natives of Belfast, and headed by Protestant traitors like Theobald Wolfe Tone, Napper Tandy, Lord Edward FitzGerald, and others, whose disloyal efforts to sever the connexion between Ireland and Great Britain, and establish an Irish Republic, are fully related by the Rev. R. R. Madden in his *Lives of the United Irishmen*. Mr. Pitt, well aware that by the enactments of 1782 Ireland was as independent of Great Britain as Great Britain was of Ireland, resolved to try and induce the Irish people, without whom he could not hope to effect a binding union, to agree to his project of consolidating the Empire. He therefore resolved to send a viceroy who was a known friend to the Catholic claims, and in the selection of Earl FitzWilliam did much to effect his object. He had another project to aid him.

We have already seen that there was a project to provide independent and sufficient maintenance for the clergy of the Roman Catholic Church in Ireland, in the Act of Union, when granting relief to the Catholics. We also find the four Archbishops of Armagh, Dublin, Tuam, and Cashel, and several other prelates, were willing to accept this; and though I believe in the time of O'Connell some effort was made to ascertain their wishes, and he found that they would not accept any provision—of course so much must depend on the mode of settling this matter—he did not push the subject. It was very different in the last century, when Catholics were enslaved. But in this just and salutary measure Mr. Pitt was obstructed by the Protestant Ascendancy party, who so long had held their fellow-countrymen in bondage because they were Catholics. Though Lord FitzWilliam before leaving London was desired not to oppose the Catholic claim, he found the Beresford faction too strong to be resisted; and, as we have seen, Mr. Pitt was obliged to recall him, on the pretext that the viceroy had misunderstood his instructions, to the grief of the nation and especially the Catholic portion. Earl FitzWilliam was recalled, and replaced by a nobleman of quite the opposite feelings, who at once became the idol of the Ascendancy party, and in this way goaded the misguided people into rebellion..

The difference of opinion of the two Parliaments on the question of the regent's power was thus avoided, when another difference arose. By the removal of commercial restraints the Irish claimed the right of exporting their goods into foreign countries as freely as the English, and Irish wool was sent to Portugal. But the Portuguese declined to receive it, and so the Irish Parliament addressed the king to coerce the Portuguese Government to make no distinction between Irish and English wool.

Those important differences suggested to the

sagacious mind of Pitt, then prime minister, the
necessity of a Union. The necessity of making
Ireland a republic by the aid of French invasion was
conceived by the Ulster Republicans—men of great
talents and influence, but imbued with hostility to
the throne and constitution of Great Britain.[1] We
shall see, later on, the efforts Mr. Pitt's well-chosen
viceroy, Lord Cornwallis, made to induce the people
of Ireland to consent to the Union, without which
the king said it would be nothing.

[1] *Hist. Rev.*, by Ball, p. 162 ; *Leckie's History*, vol. iv. p.
520 ; *Speeches of Sir Robert Peel*, vol. ii. p. 425.

CHAPTER XVIII.

CHANGE OF VICEROY IN 1778—THE PROPOSED REGENCY.

Duke of Rutland Viceroy — Viceroy's Salary increased — Anecdote of a proper Rebuke—Mr. Pitt's Letter to the Duke—Death of the Duke—His Successor the Marquis of Buckingham—Insanity of King George III.—Mr. Pitt determines to restrict the Power of the Prince of Wales as Regent—The Irish Parliament grant unlimited Power —Action of the Viceroy—Gratitude of the Prince—The Round Robin—Recall of Marquis of Buckingham—Pitt's Union Policy.

DURING the viceroyalty of the young Duke of Rutland, the salary of the viceroy was increased from £16,000 to £20,000 a year, and great festivities prevailed both at the Castle and Viceregal Lodge. The duke was of a most convivial disposition, and he was devoted to the drinking habits then so prevalent. An anecdote of water-drinking by one of the courtiers who attended a Castle banquet, met with so proper a rebuke from the viceroy, it deserves to be recorded. When the finger-glasses were placed on the dinner-table, that used by the duchess, a very beautiful young lady, was seized, after she had dipped her fingers, by one of the party, Sir Hercules Langishe, who, by way of testifying his admiration for the duchess, proceeded to drink the contents of the vessel.

This naturally attracted attention, and the viceroy was resolved to administer a rebuke to the perpetrator of this violation of decorum. "By jove, sir," he said, "you are in luck. The duchess washes her feet to-night, and I'll tell her waiting-maid to keep the water for you."

Viceroy Duke of Rutland told the Right Rev. Dr. Wilson, Bishop of Llandaff, that the man who would propose a union between Ireland and Great Britain would be tarred and feathered. Yet that the measure of union was in contemplation appears from letters now discovered. In 1784, the Duke of Rutland wrote to Pitt that, without a union, Ireland would not be connected with Great Britain twenty years longer. This intimation from the viceroy, whose convivial habits brought him into association with men well acquainted with the popular feeling, and as we know, *in vino veritas*, showed Pitt that the desire to have free trade was very deep-seated, and he was too sagacious a statesman not to try and gain favour with the Irish merchants. Accordingly, on the 6th January 1785, Mr. Pitt wrote a most important letter to the Duke of Rutland. He states the Cabinet agreed to give Ireland, not only full equality with England in all matters of trade and commerce, but more than equality advantages. Notwithstanding this, the commercial propositions of Pitt were not favourably received by the Irish Parliament.

It might have been well if the viceroy had used a little more water and less wine, for he died while in office on the 24th October 1787, in his thirty-fourth year of life. During the administration of his successor, the Marquis of Buckingham, a direct collision took place between the Parliament of Great Britain and that of Ireland, which, I think, was one of the principal reasons which induced Mr. Pitt to determine on the extinction of the Irish, by merging it in the Parliament of Great Britain, and thus form a united Parliament.

The occasion was the insanity of his Majesty George III. In 1788, the king was unable to rule, and the Prince of Wales was to be appointed regent, but his Royal Highness had so many friends among the Whig party, led by Charles James Fox, that he resolved his Royal Highness should have conditions imposed upon him: that the care of the royal person, the management of the household, appointment of officers and servants, should be vested in the queen; that his Royal Highness should only exercise his power in a limited way in granting offices or pensions, and not any dignity of peerage, except to his Majesty's issue. The Prince of Wales was very indignant at this proposal of the prime minister, and had a very spirited refusal despatched to Mr. Pitt.[1]

---

[1] The important correspondence is published in the *Lives of the Lord Chancellors of Ireland*, vol. ii. pp. 179-192. The reply of the prince is supposed to have been written by Edmund Burke.

Notwithstanding the repugnance of the prince, Mr. Pitt had sufficient influence with the British Parliament that his plan was carried. The Bill introduced on February 1st was passed on the 12th of that month, 1789.

When the state of the king's health was made known to the Irish, Mr. FitzHerbert stated the Irish Government intended to create the Prince of Wales regent by a Bill. This Mr. Ponsonby regarded as unconstitutional, and Mr. Connolly moved, and Mr. Ponsonby seconded, the following motion:—" That it is the opinion of this committee that a humble address be presented to his Royal Highness the Prince of Wales, to request him to take upon himself the government of this realm during the continuation of his Majesty's present indisposition, and no longer; and under the style and title of Prince Regent of Ireland, in the name of his Majesty, to exercise and administer, according to the laws and constitution of this kingdom, all regal power, jurisdiction, and prerogative to the Crown and Government thereof belonging."

Thus the two Parliaments were at variance. While the British Parliament conferred only a limited regency on the Prince of Wales, the Irish conferred unrestricted power.

The language of the Attorney-General[1] (Fitz-Gibbon) is worth quoting at this time in

[1] FitzGibbon, afterwards lord chancellor and Earl of Clare.

reference to Irish Home Rule. He maintained "that the Crowns of England and Ireland are inseparably and indissolubly united, and the Irish Parliament totally independent of the British Parliament. The first position is your security—the second is your freedom; and when gentlemen talk any other language, they either tend to the separation of the Crowns or the subjugation of your Parliament—they invade either your security or your liberty. Further, the only security of your liberty is your connexion with Great Britain; and gentlemen who risk breaking that connexion must make up their minds to a union. GOD FORBID I SHOULD EVER SEE THAT DAY; but if ever the day on which a separation shall be attempted may come, I shall not hesitate to embrace a union rather than a separation."[1]

A division carried the address by a large majority, and a deputation waited on the lord-lieutenant to require him to forward it to the prince. But his Excellency said he could not do so consistently with his position, "as it proposed to invest his Royal Highness with power to take upon him the government of the realm before he shall be entitled by law to do so." This gave great offence to the prince's friends in Ireland, and some strong censures on his conduct were expressed in and out of the Irish Parliament. That the prince was most grateful for the action of the Irish Parliament, is expressed in a letter from Mr.

[1] *Lives of the Lord Chancellors of Ireland*, vol. ii. p. 185.

Pelham[1] to Grattan, dated 19th February 1789: "I trust that our friends in Ireland, who have done themselves so much honour by their conduct, will not be dispirited by the tricks and intrigues of the Pitt faction. I have not time to express to you how strongly the prince is affected by the confidence and attachment of the Irish Parliament. I saw him at Carlton House, and he ordered me to write to you, but I have only time to say, in his own words, 'TELL GRATTAN THAT I AM A MOST DETERMINED IRISHMAN.'"

It is a proof of the little faith to be placed in such declarations, that this most determined Irishman of 1789 could scarcely be prevailed on to pass the Catholic Emancipation Bill of 1829, but no doubt party wars made him forget the indiscretions of his youth. The question at issue between the two Houses of Parliament was settled by the recovery of the king on 9th March 1789. A vote of censure having been passed on the lord-lieutenant gave great offence, as did the course taken by the majority of the Irish House of Commons in opposing the policy of Mr. Pitt. A rumour being spread that all places and pensions held by members of Parliament in Opposition, at the pleasure of the Crown, should be withdrawn, and the holders made *victims of their vote*, a resolution settled by Mr. Grattan declared, "That if any one of the subscribing persons shall, in consequence of his conduct upon the regency question, or upon the measures

---
[1] Lord Chichester.

necessary to be taken in consequence thereof, be deprived of his office or pension, or shall be made, as is threatened, *the victim of his vote,* we agree we will not accept of such office or pension for ourselves or any other person, and that we shall consider such deprivation, dismissal, or the rendering such individual the victim of his vote, as a reprobation of our political conduct an attack upon public principle and the independence of Parliament; and that any administration taking or persevering in any such steps is not entitled to our confidence, and shall not receive our support."

This pledge was signed by no less than fifty-six peers and members of the House of Commons, and called the Round Robin.

Notwithstanding these threats, then offers to abandon the intention of dismissing the hostile officials if they would support Mr. Pitt, and finding stubborn resistance, the project was effected, and officials of the highest rank, and pensions to the amount of £20,000 a year, were forfeited by the Irish patriotic party.

CHAPTER XIX.

1795–1798.

Viceroyalty of Marquis Camden and Marquis Cornwallis—Lord Camden Viceroy in March 1795—Triumph of the Protestant Ascendancy Party—The Beresfords—Gloomy Prospects—Conflict at the Diamond—The Irish Rebel—The French in Bantry Bay in 1796—Change of Viceroy—Expedition failed—The landing in Killala in 1798—Withdrawal of Nationalist Members from Parliament—Encounter at Castlebar—Defeat of the British Troops—The Viceroy marches against the French—The Surrender at Ballinamuck—The Tour of the Viceroy to procure Addresses in favour of the Union—Mr. Plunket's Statement of how the Addresses were procured.

ON the 31st March 1795, the Earl, subsequently Marquis Camden, succeeded the popular viceroy, Lord FitzWilliam. His position soon gave confidence to the Ascendancy party, and again the Beresfords were in the possession of power to oppress and harass the Catholics. This sudden recall of the only viceroy who, for centuries, had gained the confidence and won the affections of the Irish people, and who, during his three months' brief tenure of office, had done a great deal to make British rule submitted to throughout Ireland, was attended with sad results. Gloom fell like a pall upon the nation, and hopes, which rose bright during the tenure of office of Lord FitzWilliam, were soon to be quenched in blood.

On the 21st September 1795, the Protestants of Ulster, under the name of Peep-o'-Day-Boys, came into collision with a party of Catholics calling themselves Defenders, and had a pitched battle at a place named the Diamond, in which the Protestant party were victorious, and henceforward are known as Orangemen.[1]

The elements tended to defeat the Armada; so the same power prevented the landing of the French troops procured by the offices of Theobold Wolfe Tone, who, on the 24th December 1796, arrived in Bantry Bay. Had this formidable expedition landed on Irish soil, the country would certainly have secured freedom at last from British rule. The fleet consisted of no less than seventeen line-of-battle ships, thirteen frigates, and thirteen sloops. They had on board an army of 14,000 men, 45,000 stand of arms, with artillery and military stores. The land troops were commanded by Generals Hoche and Grouchy; the fleet by Admiral Bouvet. The weather was so stormy no effort was made to land

---

[1] *Catechism of Irish History*, p. 487. Surely history repeats itself. The hopes of Ireland for Home Rule were high during the viceroyalty of the Earl of Aberdeen in 1886. By the advent of Lord Salisbury to power Lord Aberdeen is replaced by the Marquis of Londonderry, and again the Orangemen of Ulster commenced destroying Catholic life and property.

the troops, and thus the British rule was preserved in Ireland.

On landing in Bantry Bay the French intended proceeding to Cork. The Protestants and Catholics of that city, who seldom agree on any point, are both alive to the great commercial benefits they would derive from it.[1]

The mayor of Cork at this time was Philip Allan. It is related of the mayor, in 1796, that when it was reported the French ships of war were in Bantry Bay, he so lost his senses, that when writing to the then viceroy, praying for troops to defend the city, he said: "To give your Excellency some idea of the way all loyal men are prepared to resist invasion, while I write I hold *a pistol in each hand and a sword in the other.*"

The Roman Catholic bishop, the Right Rev. Dr. Moylan, who was under the impression that the emancipation of the Catholics was part of the Union, strongly supported the measure. His experience of the intolerant spirit of bigotry and hostility of the Irish House of Commons, as shown in the divisions, or by other moderate measures of relief, to the intolerable grievances under which the Catholics of Great Britain and Ireland then laboured, when the measure had only 14 for, to 143 against even the smallest concession, induced the respected Bishop Moylan to write the letter in the Castlereagh Correspondence, approving of the Union as the only chance of obtaining Catholic Emancipation.

[1] Gibson's *History of Cork*, vol. ii. p. 259.

Some able statesmen approved of the Union. Montesquieu, the eminent French statesman and writer, strongly recommended the Union. Writing to Lord Charlemont, he thus expressed his opinion: "Were I an Irishman I would certainly wish for a union between England and Ireland, and as a great lover of liberty I sincerely desire it, and for this plain reason, that an inferior country connected with one much more superior in force, can never be certain of constitutional freedom unless she has by her representatives a proportional share in the legislature of the superior country."[1]

As we have seen, a very important difference arose on the illness of King George III. Mr. Pitt and the ministry of that time prepared to appoint the Prince of Wales regent, with limited powers, while the Irish Parliament considered the prince regent should have the same power as the king; and there being no mode of reconciling the two Parliaments, the difference would have gone on had not the king recovered, and for the time the controversy ended.

When the Belfast united Irish traitors were pressing on the French Government, the sending a force to Ireland had effect, and it is hard to say what might have been the result had not the same Divine Providence which defeated the Spanish Armada protected the Irish loyalists in 1797. The rebellion of 1798 decided Pitt, and accordingly he resolved to consolidate the empire by binding

[1] Hardy's *Life of Charlemont*, i. p. 70.

Ireland with Great Britain. The fact that Ireland was threatened by invasion from without, and actual rebellion within, must tend to excuse Mr. Pitt from his resolution to effect the union. No doubt the means he adopted, bribery and corruption, showed the venality of the class who then were the members of the Irish Parliament—the Protestant aristocracy. The desire to share in the plunder was not wholly confined to the parliamentary supporters of the Government.[1]

There appears to have been some promise held out that the British minister would not press the Union contrary to the wishes of the Irish people. It was therefore Mr. Pitt's instructions to the viceroy, Lord Cornwallis, to use his best exertions to show that the principal portion of the inhabitants were favourable; and I now proceed to show how indefatigable his Excellency was in attempting to fulfil the desires of Mr. Pitt.

No place was too obscure to be visited, no result too low to be counted, no threat too vile to be refrained from; the counties were legally convened by the high sheriffs; every attempt was made to procure the suffrages of the independent portion of the community; public addresses were sought for from petty villages.

Thinkel stated:—"After employing your military commanders, the concentrated activity of life and death, to hunt the rebels against the constituted authorities; after squeezing the lowest dregs

[1] *Hist. Review* by Ball, p. 170.

of a population of near five millions, you obtained about five thousand signatures, three-fourths of whom affixed their names in surprise, terror, or total ignorance of the subject; and after all this canvass of the people, and after all this corruption wasted on the Parliament, and after all your boasting, after abusing the names of the dead, and forging the signatures of the living; after polling the inhabitants of the gaol, and calling out against Parliament the suffrages of those who dare not come in to sign until they got their protection in their pockets; after employing the revenue officers to threaten the publican that he should be marked as a victim, and the agent to terrify the shivering tenant with the prospect of his turf-bog being withheld if he did not sign the address, and private signatures smuggled from public counters,—and how procured? By the influence of absentee landlords—not over the affections, but over the terrors of their tenantry; by grasping agents and revenue officers. And after all this mummery had been exhausted; after the lustre of royalty had been tarnished by this vulgar intercourse with the lowest rabble; after every spot had been selected where a paltry address could be secured, and every place avoided where a manly courage would have refused to aid the efforts of the viceroy." Ireland then had numerous members ever ready to sell their comrades who blindly trusted them.

Every man of influence who supported the Union was gratified, either by elevation in rank if a peer, by a peerage if a commoner, or by money if he preferred. The compensation money paid for disfranchising and decreasing the opposition in the boroughs amounted to one million two hundred thousand pounds—"Paid by the people," said Grattan, "for getting themselves turned out of Parliament." The price paid to patrons of boroughs was fifteen thousand pounds for each. The Earl of Shannon had the patronage of four boroughs in County Cork, which were worth sixty thousand pounds.

Lord Castlereagh, the chief secretary, who spent a large amount of money in bribing and distributing places and pensions to secure a majority in the Houses of Lords and Commons, brought forward Mr. Pitt's measure, for there was an idea, and perhaps a well-grounded one, that some violent demonstration, such as I have previously narrated, might arise.

The position of Foster, the Speaker, who to the last was hostile to the Union, but now constrained by his duty, was a painful one. When the House met, the sad aspect of almost every one denoted that a dissolution was at hand. The galleries were full, but no longer thronged; but no longer were they to be charmed with the eloquence and talent that so long resounded in the chamber. After some routine business, the order of the day for the third reading of the Bill for the legislative Union was carried.

CHAPTER XX.

1798–1800.

Marquis Cornwallis Viceroy—His Qualification for Office—Dialogue with Mr. Howard of Corby—Ignorance of the British Ministry respecting the Irish People—City of Cork supports the Union—Rebellion of 1798—Grattan and others Absent from Parliament—On his Return attacked by Mr. Corry—Grattan's scathing Reply—On Bill for O'Donnell's Motion—The Speaker appeals to the House—Effort of the Viceroy in support of the Bill—Heart of a popular Tumult—The Speaker puts the Question—Carried.

IN June 1798 another change of viceroys took place. Marquis Camden, whose administration was well calculated to promote the scheme of Mr. Pitt, and goad the Irish into disaffection to British rule, having effected his object, was recalled, and replaced by a very different nobleman, Marquis Cornwallis. He had served in the British army, but his campaign in America had not reflected any lustre on British arms. Perhaps he hoped to regain his lost laurels in Ireland, when on 20th June he assumed the duties of lord-lieutenant.

There is no doubt that Mr. Pitt selected the best

man of his party to act as viceroy, in the Marquis Cornwallis. His affable manners and desire to please made him as popular as any nobleman in his position could possibly be; and those who opposed his political views could not help liking him personally. He was an attached friend to one of the heads of the great Catholic house of Howard—Henry Howard of Corby, who in 1799 was quartered in Dublin with his regiment. His son, the late Philip Howard, Esq. of Corby Castle, member for Carlisle, kindly sent me the minutes of a conversation between his father and the viceroy, as follows:—" December 11th, 1799. Dined, Park. After dinner sat by Lord Cornwallis. Addressing him on the subject of the state of Ireland between Catholic and Protestant, I said 'that I thought, from what I perceived of the state of men's minds, that the best and most useful part of the Government was to hinder the people cutting each other's throats.' He replied, 'That, unfortunately, was not what the Government had done here.' I said, 'I thought that justice began to be done on that score, which, when I came first, was by no means the case.' This brought on the subject of Union, which ' he thought the only remedy and means of doing that which, left to them here, would never be done.' I said, 'With respect to the Catholics, as it appeared to be an object to conciliate them, that they should be an object of union, that without this the Union was nothing.' He replied, 'Certainly the Union without it is nothing.'"

The correspondence of the viceroy shows how well he understood the character of the men who were most strongly promoting the Union. In a letter to General Ross he says: "The ministry knows very little about this country, and they take an interested, violent, and prejudiced party, who call themselves friends to England and the Protestant interests, for the people of Ireland. If a successor was to be appointed who should, as almost all former lord-lieutenants have done, throw himself into the hands of this party, no advantage would be derived from the Union. He was anxious to reform the Government; he disliked the vile crew. However, they must be treated with management and attention, and I have been so fortunate as to retain in a great degree their good-will, at the same time to have acquired the confidence of the Catholics."

It is strange that at this time, when the country most needed the influence of the comparatively few patriots in Parliament, they should think fit to abandon their trust. Grattan and others, who felt they could not carry the measure they deemed requisite for the relief of the Catholics, returned to their country seats and thus gave the Government full sway to act as they chose.[1]

Again negotiations were entered into for another French expedition to aid the rebellion of the United Irishmen, and this time the place of landing was Killala Bay, in the west of Ireland. Here, on the 22nd August 1798, the French, under General

[1] For explanation see Grattan's reply to Corry.

Humbert, to the number of eleven thousand, landed. They marched on Castlebar, and defeated the British troops under General Lord Lake.

The news of this defeat having reached Dublin, the viceroy, Marquis Cornwallis, at once set out with such troops as he could muster. Humbert with his small force kept the British troops in motion for some days, but at length, being surrounded by thirty thousand men, on the 8th September the French surrendered themselves prisoners of war at Ballinamuck. Weakened by rebellion and disheartened by civil dissension, Ireland now seemed incapable of offering any effectual resistance to Mr. Pitt's project of uniting the legislative body of Ireland with that of Great Britain; some show of popular feeling on the part of the Irish in favour of this measure being deemed requisite.

The Bill for the legislative union between Great Britain and Ireland was moved by Lord Castlereagh. He used no superfluous-words, moved it as a commonplace notice, and then resumed his seat. The House, indeed, was visibly affected, and many members withdrew before the fatal question was put from the chair. After a brief pause, the Speaker rose, and, as if unable to speak, again sat down. But the bitter task had to be performed, and with that air of dignity which ever distinguished his position, and after a brief survey of the doomed House, he pronounced the fervid words, " As many as are of opinion this Bill do pass, say Aye; the contrary say No." The affirmative was uttered in low yet decisive tones, but in number indisputable. Another pause, and again the voice of the Speaker seemed inaudible. After a brief interval, as though gaining strength to speak what required to be spoken, with his eyes turned away from the Bill he held in his hand, he declared the result was "the Ayes have it;" and, as if getting rid of some hateful object, he flung the Bill upon the table, and threw himself back in his chair as though exhausted by the effort.

In a short time the members left, and thus the House of Commons was abandoned to become the Bank of Ireland.

CHAPTER XXI.

1800.

Hopes of Popular Dissent rejected — Viceroy's Efforts to procure Public Approval—His abortive Efforts to obtain Public Approval—The Bill in the House of Commons—Startling Proposal from the Gallery — Last Sitting moved by Lord Castlereagh—Distress of the Speaker (Foster)—The Members on the Question—The Ayes have it—The Bill in the Lords—The Chancellor's Speech —Praise of the Viceroy—The Lords' Debate—The Act passed—Protest of Dissentient Peers—Intended Projects for supporting Catholic Clergy—Act of Compensation for Boroughs—Popular Hits at corrupt Members.

BUT the Union met with strong, if unavailing resistance. On the 8th June 1800, when the question was put in the House of Commons, "That this Bill be engrossed," a sturdy member named O'Donnell moved, "That instead of being engrossed it should be burnt." Mr. Tighe seconded this motion, and several members insisted on the motion being put to the House. The Speaker (Foster) appealed to the House as to the propriety of putting such a question, when the Government party demanded it should not, that it was most improper, and any member persisting in pressing it incurred a vote of censure; and a scene of great confusion arose. The galleries had to be cleared, and when order was restored, the Speaker said, "This point was novel, and without precedent." He thought the motion might be made at a proper time, and was not censurable as an insult, but it could not supersede the question, which he put accordingly.[1]

The history of the Rebellion of 1798 forms no part of my narrative, save so far as it prevented the measure of the Union. That its origin and progress was perfectly known to the Irish executive, there is not a shadow of doubt; and assuredly, with the means the viceroy, Lord Camden, had at his disposal, and the great military force at his command, he could have nipped the conspiracy in the bud before it assumed the alarming dimensions it soon reached. Providence fought with the cause of British rule, as in the reign of Queen Elizabeth.

It is worthy of note that in his violent anti-Irish speech, the chancellor accused the Opposition peers of using undue influence and bribery to incite the people against the Union. We shall presently see with what bad grace such a charge came from the Treasury bench against noblemen, who denied that they ever resorted to such conduct. The strong opposition throughout the country gave great offence to the Irish Government. In a letter to General Ross, dated 28th February 1800, the lord-lieutenant says: " The Opposition here still remains

---

[1] *Lives of the Lord Chancellors of Ireland*, vol. ii. p. 268, and note at foot.

united, and seem determined to employ every means to protract the business, while we feel the greatest difficulty to call forth any exertion, or even to procure a tolerable attendance from our languid friends. The Speaker[1] plays all the game for them, and counts the House exactly at four, before which time all the opponents take care to withdraw, and will not suffer any man to stir to call in such careless members as may be in the lobby or porch."[2]

While the debate on the Union was progressing in the House of Commons, the anxiety of the people to learn who were the friends and foes of Irish patriotism thronged the galleries. It would seem as if the same strictness which regulates admission to the Speaker or the Strangers' Gallery of the Imperial Parliament was not observed; for one evening the House was electrified by a loud voice from the gallery calling, "Now let the greatest assassin take the chair!" The Speaker at once ordered the arrest of the offender, who was soon in custody of the serjeant-at-arms, and brought to the bar of the House. He behaved in so violent a manner he was committed to Newgate. Here, sober reason having returned, he was ashamed of his conduct, and, having addressed a most penitent apology to the House, was discharged after being in prison nearly two months.

In order to secure a majority for the Union, the

[1] Right Hon. J. Foster.
[2] *Cornwallis Correspondence*, vol. iii. p. 154.

flood-gates of corruption were opened. Lord Cornwallis, the lord-lieutenant, writing to his friend, General Ross of Bladensburgh, says: "My occupation is negotiating and jobbing. How I hate myself every hour from being engaged in this dirty work! How I long to kick those I am obliged to court! Castlereagh distributed to secure votes, twenty peerage, twenty advances of rank in the peerage, seven judgeships, over two hundred salaried places, and over two million of pounds sterling cash paid.

Meanwhile the minions of the Government beset members in any position, high or low, and so the members of the House of Commons, the most numerous portion being bought by the ministers, in a manner deserving of the reproach of a prime minister,[1] who was justified in stigmatising the conduct of his predecessors *as blackguards*, outnumbered the band of patriots who resisted the disastrous measure. On the 11th June 1800, the Commons of Ireland sat. They could not be called a representative assembly. English officials were smuggled into seats to vote as they were ordered. They were placed to repeal the Acts of 1782, which, I believe, were wrung from a terrified ministry with the fixed resolution to overrule its enactments at a fitting time, and that time was now come. The Parliament House was closely invested by a large military force.

The Marquis Cornwallis was soon busy in pro-

[1] Right Hon. W. E. Gladstone.

moting the legislative union. On 7th February 1800, the chancellor, Earl of Clare, in the House of Lords, had delivered the message in favour of this Bill, which was at once taken into consideration. On the 10th of the month, the chancellor introduced the measure, in a speech which, when put into type, numbered a hundred pages. It was a sort of Irish history detailing all her calamities and civil strifes; it was full of misstatements, abusing the native Irish, assailing the Roman Catholics, flattering the English. Those peers whom he suspected of national leanings he assailed — Lord Downshire and Lord Charlemont especially; and Grattan, with his party, of course, were objects of his attack.

This was the sort of harangue to win praise from the Irish Castle officials. In a letter to the Duke of Portland, the viceroy wrote: "I am to state to your Grace that the chancellor exerted his great abilities in a speech of four hours, which produced the greatest surprise and effect on the Lords and on the audience, which was uncommonly numerous."

In support of the measure spoke Lords Glentworth,[1] Kilwarden, Chief Justice of the King's Bench;[2] Lord Carleton, Chief Justice of the Common Pleas; Lords Donaghmore, Longford, Glandore, and the Archbishop of Cashel. Those peers who spoke against the Union were—the Marquis of

[1] Pery, Earl of Limerick.
[2] Killed during the Emmett revolt in 1803.

Downshire, the Earl of Charlemont, Lords Farnham, Dillon, Powerscourt, and Sunderlin.

The Bill seems to have gone at once to the Lords, who by a majority of 76 for, to 13 against it, passed it on the 12th June, and on the 1st August it received the royal assent. On the following day the viceroy, in a speech from the throne, pronounced the extinction of the Irish Parliament. We are not aware if any one called out, as the old Scotch peer did when the Union between England and Scotland deprived Edina of her ancient "legislative powers," "Sae there's an end to the auld sang." A strongly-worded protest from the unbribed and unbought members of the peerage of Ireland will serve to recall to the minds of their descendants how nobly their fathers acted on this sad occasion.

The protest, in eleven sections, dated 13th June 1800, thus concludes: "Because the arguments made use of in favour of the Union—namely, that the sense of the nation is in its favour—we know to be untrue; and as the ministers have declared that they would not press the measure against the sense of the people, and the people have pronounced decidedly, and under all difficulties, their judgment against it, we have, together with the sense of the country, the authority of the ministers to enter our protest against the project of union, against the yoke which it imposes, the dishonour which it inflicts, the disqualification passed upon the peerage, the stigma thereby branded on the realm, the disproportionate principle of expense it introduces, the means employed to effect it, the discontent it has excited and must continue to excite; against all these and the fatal consequences they may produce we have endeavoured to interpose our votes; and failing, we transmit to after times our names in solemn protest in behalf of the parliamentary constitution of the realm, the liberty which it secured, the trade which it protected, the connexion which it preserved, and the constitution which it supplied and formed. This we feel ourselves called upon to do in support of our characters, our honour, and whatever is left us worthy to be transmitted to our posterity.

LEINSTER.	RICHARD, BISHOP OF WA-
ARRAN.	TERFORD AND LISMORE.
MOUNTCASHEL.	POWERSCOURT.
FARNHAM.	DE VESCI.
BELMORE.	CHARLEMONT.
MASSY.	KINGSTON.
STRANGFORD.	RIVERSDALE.
GRANARD.	MEATH.
LUDLOW.	LISMORE.
MOIRA.	SUNDERLIN."
WILLIAM, BISHOP OF	
DOWN AND CONNOR.	

There is no doubt that a proposal was then made for making due provision for the bishops and clergy of the Catholic Church. They are, and have been, quite dependent on the offerings of their parishioners, and this very dependence has often the effect of compelling the clergy to adapt themselves to the wishes and actions of those people, than if independent they might not do so.

In 1799, a meeting of the bishops was held to consider a proposal from the Government to grant an independent provision to the clergy, and a document was then drawn up, signed by the four archbishops and six bishops, in which it was agreed that a provision for the Roman Catholic clergy of Ireland, competent and secured, ought to be thankfully accepted, and the regulations which it was thought proper should accompany it were laid down.[1]

Together with the Act of Union was an Act giving an enormous sum to compensate the owners of boroughs disfranchised by the Union. As the market price which was often paid for the honour and glory of being a member of Parliament for one of these boroughs was as high as £7000, and these boroughs returned two members, thus each was valued at £14,000; and as there were many such boroughs, the amount paid was £1,260,000.[2] Ireland, in the united Parliament, was to be represented by thirty-two peers, four of them to be Lords Spiritual, and twenty-eight Temporal, elected for life by their fellow Irish peers. The House of Commons was to be represented by sixty-four from the

---

[1] *Grattan's Life*, by his Son, vol. v. p. 57. *Quarterly Review*, vol. lxxvii. p. 247.

[2] *Historical Review* by Ball, p. 224.

thirty-two counties, two from each; four from Dublin and Cork, two each; one from Trinity College, and one from thirty-two cities and important boroughs— one hundred in all. The Irish population, who were aware of the wholesale bribery going on, and by shrewdly recognising the venal crew who gained access to the chief secretary by the back stair of the Castle, lost no opportunity of attacking them in the streets. They would say: "So, Mr. ———, you were paid this morning. Give us a tenpenny bit to drink your health."

To a peer: "Well, my lord, you made a good bargain. You were right not to sell your country too cheap."

"Three cheers for Sir William. He bargained to be a lord, but there was no lord for him."

"Here's Harry D—— G———, boys! How much did they mark on your brief, Harry?" This old parliamentary lawyer is reported to have replied to the indignant inquiry, "Will you sell your country?" "Thank God I have a country to sell."

No wonder the high-minded and noble Marquis Cornwallis was disgusted at having to bargain with such rascals. No wonder, as he said, he longed to kick those he was obliged to court. We have had, alas! in our day, men equally open to the influence of corruption, and let us pray that we have seen the last of those, when we return our Parliament once more to College Green.

APPENDICES.

APPENDIX I.

The Parliament House—The Exterior—Anecdote of the Statues—A New Order of Architecture—Interior—The Houses of Lords and Commons—Cost of Erection—Floored after the Union—Sale to the Bank of Ireland.

THE Parliament House of Dublin has justly been regarded as one of the finest buildings in Europe. It occupies the position in the south side of the city where Westmoreland Street connects the city with College Green. This splendid structure was commenced in A.D. 1729, during the viceroyalty of Lord Carteret, and though some doubt exists as to the name of the architect who furnished the original plan, it is confidently stated that the celebrated Gandon was employed in its erection. It is at once remarkable for its simplicity and dignity; and though harmony of style has not been preserved throughout, there is sufficient unity of design to please the most critical. When seen from Grafton Street, as has been well said, it derives all its beauty from a simple display of fine art, and is one of the few instances of form expressing true symmetry. The principal front, facing College Green, contains a stately portico, the entablature and corner surmounted by an attic, the tympanum sustaining the royal arms. From the front are spacious colonnades, forming with the centre three sides of a quadrangle enclosing a courtyard. Over the front is a colossal statue of Hibernia, with statues emblematic of Commerce and Fidelity.

A stranger to Dublin, driving on an Irish jaunting car, inquired of the driver "if he knew who these statues represented."

"Oh yes, your honour!" promptly replied the driver. "Thim's the Twelve Apostles."

"Why," remarked the stranger, "there are only three."

"Oh, shure, you wouldn't expect all the gintlemen to stand out in the could at the same time; so you see they take the post in turn."

The height of the building, enriched with basement of rustic stonework, joins the eastern and western fronts with the principal entrance. These are relieved by niches placed at regular intervals between columns, and surmounted by a rich cornice and entablature. This portion of the building is of the simple, and what might be termed severe Ionic order of architecture; while the portion standing in Westmoreland Street, and six pillars with tympanum, is of the Corinthian order. Here are statues of Fortitude, Justice, and Liberty. This portico formed the entrance to the House of Lords; and it is said that during its erection some critic inquired of the architect, "Why he disturbed the harmony of the Ionic by the incongruity of the Corinthian pillars."

"Oh, you mistake," was the witty reply. "This is altogether a new order of architecture."

"And what do you call that order?" inquired the critic.

"*The Order of the Irish House of Lords,*" was the very intelligible reply.

The House of Commons is thus described by one of its most observant members:[1] "Whoever has seen the interior of the Irish House of Commons must have admitted it as one of the most chaste and classic models of architecture. A perfect rotunda with Ionic pilasters enclosed a corridor which ran round the interior. The cupola of immense height bestowed a magnificence which could rarely be

---

[1] Sir Jonah Barrington, *Personal Sketches*.

surpassed; while a gallery, supported by columns divided into compartments, and accommodating seven hundred spectators, commanded an uninterrupted view of the chamber.

"This gallery on every important debate was filled by the superior order of society in Dublin, the first row being occupied by ladies, not put behind a grate, as in Westminster, where they are very inconveniently located for seeing or hearing; but in Dublin they not only saw and heard what was going forward, but were seen themselves—no mean consideration where youth, beauty, grace, and fashionable attire were displayed."

To suit the altered requirements when the Parliament House was *improved* into the Bank of Ireland, this grand hall of the people's representatives was turned from a rotunda into a square, and now the only portion unaltered is the House of Lords. It is of course much smaller than was required for the Commons, and the walls are covered with tapestry representing the battle of the Boyne and the siege of Londonderry, both emblematic of Protestant triumphs. A statue of King George III. occupies a recess in which the throne was placed. It is stated that the building originally cost £90,000, but after the Union was sold to the Bank of Ireland for £40,000.

APPENDIX II.

Parliamentary Banquets peculiar to Ireland—Peers and Members of the House of Commons join in the Revelry.

Sir Jonah Barrington relates the following:—"On the day when the routine business of the budget was to be opened for the purpose of voting supplies, the Speaker invited the whole of the members to dinner in the House, in his own and the adjoining chambers. Several peers were accustomed to mix in the company; and I believe an equally happy, joyous, and convivial assemblage of legislators never were seen together. All distinction as to Government or Opposition parties was totally laid aside—harmony, wit, wine, and good humour reigning triumphant. The Speaker, clerk, chancellor of the exchequer, and a very few veteran financiers remained in the House till the necessary routine was gone through, and then joined their happy comrades, the party seldom breaking up till midnight.

"On the ensuing day the same festivities were repeated; but on the third day, when the report was to be brought up and the business to be discussed in detail, the scene totally changed: the convivialists were now metamorphosed into downright public declamatory enemies, and, ranged on opposite sides of the House, assailed each other without mercy. Every questionable item was debated, every proposition deliberately discussed, and more zealous or assiduous senators could nowhere be found than in the very members who, during two days, had appeared to commit the whole funds of the nation to the management of half a dozen arithmeticians. But all this was consonant to the national character of the individuals. Set them at table, and no men enjoyed themselves half so much; set them to business, no men ever worked with more earnestness and effect. A steady Irishman will do more in an hour when fairly engaged upon a matter which he understands, than any other countryman in two. The persons of whom I am more immediately speaking were certainly extraordinarily quick and sharp. I am, however, at the same time ready to admit that the lower orders of officials, such, for instance, as mere clerks in the public offices, exhibited no claims to a participation in the praise I have given to their superiors." [1]

[1] *Personal Sketches* by Sir J. Barrington, p. 102.

APPENDIX III.

Attendance of High Officials — The Ceremonies respecting the Viceroy — Conference between Lords and Commons — Royal Assent — Order in the Streets — Favourite Hours of Attendance in the House of Commons.

As it was the rule that the regulations observed by the English Parliament were adopted in Ireland, we may here mention the ceremony of opening the Parliament in Dublin, which we expect soon to see revived, was a very imposing one. Regiments of infantry lined the streets, and an escort of cavalry attended the viceroy and his staff. Bands played and trumpets sounded. On reaching the Parliament House, the viceroy repairs to his robing-room, puts on royal robes, and, attended by two earls, one bearing the sword of state, the other the cap of maintenance, and three noblemen's sons acting as train-bearers, he proceeded to the House of Lords. Then, after a bow to the vacant throne, he took his seat in a chair of state beneath the canopy. Until the viceroy has taken his seat, the peers, Spiritual and Temporal, stood in their places attired in their robes, uncovered. On the viceroy being seated they took their seats.

Conferences.

Conference between the Lords and Commons was as follows :—When the Commons sought a conference with the peers, they sent their usher to inform the Lords, who, after disposing of any business on which they were engaged, sent for the members of the House of Commons, who, on entering the House of Lords, stood at the lower end of the chamber. Then the lord chancellor, with any of the peers who pleased, rose and went to the middle of the bar where the leader of the Commons with the members stood. Having bowed thrice, the usher delivered his message to the chancellor, who thereon returned to his place, and the Commons having retired, the usher stated what the message was for.

APPENDIX IV.

Procedure during the Session.

The Lords sent for the Commons, who, re-entering, made their obeisance to the peers, and the answer of the Lords was given by the lord chancellor from his seat on the woolsack. The usher of the black rod waited outside the bar, and spoke there when required. The serjeant-at-arms waited in an adjoining room until summoned. None were allowed to be present at the debates in the House of Lords but sons of peers, and persons required to be present.

Mode of giving the Royal Assent.

When Bills had passed both Houses, and only wanted the assent of the Crown, the manner was thus:—The lord chancellor, kneeling, conferred with the viceroy, and they, standing on the right of the chair of state, commanded the usher of the black rod to acquaint the House of Commons it was his excellency's pleasure they should attend immediately at the House of Lords. Having obeyed the summons, they were conducted to the bar, and the Speaker, after a speech, read the titles of the Bills ready for the royal assent. The Bills were then delivered at the bar by the Speaker to the clerk of the Parliament, who brought them to the table, when the clerk of the Crown having read the Bills, the clerk of Parliament pronounced the royal assent separately for each Bill. In case of supplies or Bills concerning revenue, the assent ran thus: " Le Roy remercie ses bons sujets, accepti leur benevolence et ainsi les veut." When the Bills were not money Bills, the words were: " Le Roy le veut," or " Soit fait comme il est desire." His excellency then withdrew in the same state, and the Commons having retired, headed by the Speaker, returned to their House, and the Lords adjourned.

APPENDICES. 185

Order in the Streets.

Great care was taken to keep the streets as free as possible from noise or obstruction during the sitting of Parliament. Hackney vehicles were prevented from coming to the entrance doors, and the lord mayor, by proclamation, forbade all drivers of carts, cars, or drays to pass, repass, or go through the streets in front of the House, from 11 A.M. to 5 P.M. during the sitting of Parliament, in order to prevent stoppages and obstruction to the people resorting thereto.[1]

Divisions.

A very great difference in the regulations of the sittings was observed between the Irish and English Parliaments. In Ireland the divisions were public, and the names of the members who voted were published immediately after each division, so that their constituents could see how they voted. In England, on the contrary, strangers withdrew from the galleries, and for the time no one knows how the members vote. It may be said that the public have a right to know if the trust reposed in their representatives is fairly exercised, and the Irish was the more constitutional practice.

Payment of Members and Hours of Sitting.

In Ireland as well as in England, the State considered the time devoted to their public interests by their representatives in the House of Commons should be recompensed. We learn from Mr. Jenning's able and interesting work, that by statute 16th Edward II., in England the rate of wages was only 2s. 6d. for a knight of the shire, and 2s. for a citizen or burgher. We were more liberal in Ireland, for we allowed—

Knights of the shire,	£0 13 4	per day
Members for cities,	0 10 0	,,
For boroughs,	0 3 4	,,

These sums were found so oppressive in many cases, that petitions were presented to be relieved from sending

[1] *Lives of the Lord Chancellors of Ireland,* vol. i. p. 299, in note.

representatives to Parliament, on the ground of the danger incurred during the journey, and the expense of sending a sufficient guard to insure their protection.

Time of Sitting.

In ancient times, we learn, the Irish Parliament met very early in the day.

APPENDIX V.

Statute Rolls and Journals.

The statute rolls of the Irish Parliament include the statutes passed by the Parliaments held in the reigns of Henry VI., Richard III., Henry VII., Henry VIII., Philip and Mary, Elizabeth and James I.

From them to the reign of George I., A.D. 1715, public and private Acts were enrolled on the same rolls, and a calendar, but an imperfect one, was made of these Acts. From 1715 to the Union in 1800, the public and private Acts were enrolled separately.

Prior to 10 Henry VII. the statute rolls are in Norman-French, then the language of the Law Courts. But from the time of Edward III. proceedings in Parliament were in the English tongue.[1]

The Journals of the Irish House of Commons commence 18th May 1619.

Hours of Attendance of the Commons.

The hours of attendance were usually from 11 A.M. to 5 P.M., and there was much more attention paid to dress and personal adornment than has been observed in the Imperial Parliament. The Irish members of the House of Commons always wore Court dress, and such as had orders of knighthood or ribbons wore them.

[1] *Lives of the Lord Chancellors of Ireland*, vol. i. p. 66.

APPENDIX VI.

Insults to Statue of King William III.—Hoax on Sir Philip Crampton, Surgeon-General.

In 1710, the statue of King William III. in College Green, Dublin, was found so bedaubed with mud as to arouse the indignation of all the zealous admirers of that monarch. The attention of the House of Commons was promptly called to this manifest token of premeditated insult; and a resolution was carried—"That it is the opinion of this House that the perpetrators of this gross indignity be punished." The lord chancellor was directed to wait on the viceroy, and complain of the persons guilty of this greatest insolence, baseness, and ingratitude, and desire his excellency the lord-lieutenant to issue a proclamation to discover the authors of this villainy, with a reward to the discoverer that they may be prosecuted and punished accordingly. The chancellor having obeyed his instructions, the viceroy issued a proclamation, and offered £100 for the discovery of the offenders. They were three students of Trinity College, Dublin, who did it for a frolic, but the consequence was no joke to them. They were expelled the university, sentenced to six months' imprisonment, and a fine of £100 each, which was subsequently reduced.

Another indignity and a more serious one was perpetrated during the present century. Some late revellers returning from a party through Dame Street found that the statue of King William III. had been removed from his horse, and was lying sorely damaged on the flags. It instantly occurred to one of the youths that a hoax might be played on the surgeon-general, Sir Philip Crampton; and one of the party, the others keeping at a distance, proceeded to Sir Philip's house in Merrion Square, and sought his services for a very high official who was just found badly wounded on the flags in Dame Street, but no one dared to remove him until he was examined by the surgeon-general. Sir

Philip lost no time in proceeding to the place indicated, and we may presume was sorely vexed at the trick which caused him to be summoned to the effigy of the conqueror of the Boyne. I do not know if the perpetrator of this affair was discovered.

APPENDIX VII.

Troubles of Speakers.

In 1642 the Speaker (Eustace) described the state of Ireland in very eulogistic terms. The viceroy, Earl of Strafford, was then in the security of the king's friendship, and the attendance of members was quite as the most bigoted Protestant could desire.

Ere long the Speaker was destined to feel the glowing pictures he painted of the state of Ireland were not all *couleur de rose*. In 1647 his cattle were taken by soldiers, and he made a complaint to the House, but the statement in the Commons' Journals is so very unintelligible, that, were it not for the order of the House, it would be incomprehensible. I copied it *verbatim* as follows:—"Mr. Speaker, That little fortune in Kildare is lost, and that was left I brought to Irishtoune   of this House, and by the gallantry of an officer of the horse, that Lieutenant Harman may command those soldiers."

"It is ordered that Lieutenant Harman do cause the troops under his command, who took the cattle from Clonliffe belonging to Sir Maurice Eustace, knight, Speaker of this House, under pretence of contribution, do forthwith bring them back and leave them at the same place from where they were taken; whereof he or they do not fail."[1]

The Speaker also got into trouble for speaking words which imputed his conniving at Roman Catholics being members of Parliament. He said, with respect to Catholics

[1] *Lives of Lord Chancellors of Ireland*, vol. i. p. 365.

declining the Protestant oath, "You need not put him to his oath; I wish we had more of them." Simon Luttrel was the member alluded to. As it appeared the conversation took place at dinner in reference to a wager, the House did not think it worth making any stir in the matter, and that the member who imputed this connivance to the Speaker should be reconciled.

The Speaker consequently called Captain Shoute to the chair and shook hands, so the affair terminated amicably.[1] When the Parliament was prorogued, the following compliment was paid to the Speaker, and entered in the Journal of the House :—

"The House understanding that there is an intention to prorogue the Parliament for some long time, and not knowing when they shall meet again, did take into their consideration the many good services performed by Sir Maurice Eustace, knight, their Speaker, unto the House, his singular affection to the English nation and public services, his earnest endeavours for the advancement of the Protestant religion, the inveterate hatred and malice of the detestable rebels, many ways declared and acted against him, and the great expense which he hath been formerly at for the honour and service of the House, and having at the present no better way of requital than to convey the memory thereof to posterity, do think fit, in manifestation of their high esteem thereof, to declare, and do hereby declare the same to be such as in all times ought to be remembered for his advantage, and do therefore order that this be entered among the Acts and Orders of this House."[2]

We have noticed the encounter in 1695 between the rival coaches of the Lord Chancellor Bolton and the Speaker Rochfort; but as the Lords did not think any insult was premeditated, the matter was allowed to drop.

Perhaps the greatest trouble was that which afflicted the last Speaker, Foster, who was coerced by his duty to the House of Commons to put the question of the Union,

[1] *Com. Jour. Ir.* vol. i. p. 373.   [2] *Ibid.* p. 374.

which he felt was alike damaging to the country and destructive of the Irish Parliament.

APPENDIX VIII.

Violent Language—Amicable Duels.

Very violent language used in the House of Commons often called for remonstrance from the Speaker.

Mr. Egan, member for the borough of Tallow, was a large bloated barrister, who roused the anger of Mr. Grattan, who made a powerful speech on the atrocities of the Paris *sans culotte* during the French Revolution. Mr. Egan, commenting on the speech of Mr. Grattan, said, "The right hon. gentleman had so dwelt on the guillotine as to cause him, Mr. Egan, to imagine that implement on the very floor of the House."

Grattan in reply said, "The hon. member had better sight than he had, but though he failed to see the guillotine he most certainly could imagine he saw the executioner."

During the last century duels were very prevalent in Ireland, and some instances of hostile meetings are recorded, both at the Irish Bar and in the Irish Parliament. A member, Sir Richard Musgrave, having written a history of the Rebellion in 1798, which gave offence to a noted duellist, some one begged he would not shoot Sir Richard until he published his next edition, which was to correct the errors in the first. "Bedad," said the duellist, "I'll take care that his next edition will be in boards."

Curran was challenged by Egan, and when on the ground, Egan complained it was not fair; "for," said the burly member, "I am as big as a haystack, while you, Curran, are not a fourth of my size."

"Then," said Curran, "we can remedy that a little. Let my size be chalked on your big body, and any hits outside this shall not count."

This ludicrous mode of arranging a duel so tickled Egan, that there was no interchange of shots.

Another amicable termination of a hostile meeting was this: One of the party taking up his position on a high road near a milestone, observed his antagonist deliberately walking away. "Where are you going, sir?" asked the other.

"Oh, to the next milestone," was the reply. This ended the duel.

There are several ancedotes related of Egan. During a contested election for Tallow he worked himself so much as to be in a heat that perspiration was visible. On seeing this Curran said, "Why, my dear Egan, I regret to see you are losing Tallow fast."

In those days duelling was the usual mode of settling all differences.

APPENDIX IX.

Tried by his Peers—The Kingston Tragedy—A Romance of the Irish Peerage.

Now that a century has nearly elapsed since the romantic events I have to relate occurred, and the grave has long closed over the mortal remains of the actors in the tragedy, I do not hesitate to give names and dates, to prove the adage that "Truth is often stranger than fiction."

The family of King, Earls of Kingston, were possessed of large estates in Ireland since the reign of Queen Elizabeth. They were created Earls of Kingston in 1768, and their estates in Munster were of such vast extent that they were said to equal the size of the county of Kildare in Ireland, or Kent in England.

Edward King, the first Earl of Kingston, had a large old mansion at Mitchelstown, since replaced by the most majestic castle ever built in Ireland. It is, in fact, now suited for a royal residence, and in the fallen fortunes of the Kingston family quite disproportionate to its present requirements. Robert, Lord Kingsborough, eldest son of this nobleman, married, in 1769, Caroline, only daughter of Richard FitzGerald, Esq., of Mount Ophaly, in the county of Kildare, by whom he had a large family of six stately sons and four blooming daughters.

The first Earl of Kingston being alive when his eldest son, Lord Kingsborough, married, the family seat at Mitchelstown was reserved by the aged earl, and the heir, Lord Kingsborough, and his family occupied a villa near London, on the banks of the Thames.

It would have been fortunate if Lord and Lady Kingsborough had confined the family circle to their own children, but, owing to their good-nature, they did not. A brother of Lady Kingsborough, who never married, when dying besought her care for his illegitimate son, and this viper was reared with the family of Lady Kingsborough, whose peace and innocence he was fated to destroy. The children, whose games he shared, in whose education he participated, were numerous—six sons and four daughters—one of whom, a very lovely girl, Mary, was the victim of his base ingratitude.

As time went on, and the sons adopted various avocations, through the influence of the Kingston family young FitzGerald obtained a commission in the army, and at the period of his violating the sanctity of the home in which he was nurtured, had reached the rank of colonel, and was a married man.

He had, unfortunately, gained the affections of one of the daughters of his benefactors, the Honourable Mary King, and he succeeded in inducing her to meet him on the road to London, where he had a post-chaise waiting, and took her away, leaving no trace of her destination. Nothing could exceed the surprise and grief of her parents when they missed their beloved child. Finding her hat and shawl by the river-side, they had the river dragged for the body, but of course without effect. Bills were printed offering large rewards for information, and the police were employed. Every means were taken to discover her—all without effect; and, to throw off any suspicion, the vile seducer called at Lord Kingsborough's every day on the bereaved parents, inquiring, what he knew was needless, "if any clue was obtained about the fate of the missing girl."

Once, some intelligence was communicated, which relieved their fears that she had committed suicide. A post-boy, who had seen the bills, informed Lord Kingsborough he had been driving a gentleman in a post-chaise from near Acton into London on the day the young lady was last seen. On the road they saw a young lady walking, and the gentleman inquired if she was going to London? She said she was. He, the gentleman, said if she had no objection to be his companion in the carriage, he would be glad to save her the walk. On this she got in, and he, the post-boy, drove them to the end of Oxford Street, where they got out; the gentleman gave him a sovereign, and he saw them turn up Tottenham Court Road.

This gave at least the assurance that Miss Mary King did not drown herself, and the most diligent search was instituted in the direction of Tottenham Court Road, Hampstead Road, Gower Street—all to no purpose. No trace could be found of Miss King. At length, after several weeks spent in unwearied but unproductive endeavours to discover her, a young girl, poorly clad, and evidently looking what she was, a lodging-house maid-of-all-work, asked to see Lady Kingsborough. On being admitted to the heart-broken mother, this girl said she believed she had discovered the missing young lady. One fully answering in every particular the description in the advertisement which she read in the newspapers had been placed in their lodging-house by a tall handsome gentleman, about six weeks ago. This young lady had the abundance of fair hair described, and on the servant entering the young lady's bedroom that morning, she found her with a pair of scissors cutting off all her beautiful hair. This made the girl suspect she was the missing lady who was described in the newspapers. The lodging-house maid had proceeded thus far in her narrative when the footman announced Colonel FitzGerald, who came with his usual hypocritical inquiry, little thinking who he should find with Lady Kingsborough. The moment he entered the room, the lodging-house maid exclaimed, "Oh, my lady! that's the very gentleman who brought the young lady to our house!" Confounded at the discovery, the ungrateful scoundrel rushed from the house with such speed he forgot to take his hat. Lord Kingsborough was at once sent for, his carriage ordered, and, with the servant maid to direct the coachman, drove as fast as the horses could go to the house in a quiet lane near Gray's Inn Road, where he found the unhappy girl. Feeling she had better be placed at once out of the reach of her vile betrayer, after liberally rewarding the lodging-house maid, he brought his daughter across the Channel, and placed her with her maid in the ancestral castle of Mitchelstown, County Cork.

While Lord Kingsborough was absent in Ireland, his son, Colonel King, sent a friend, Major Wood, to challenge Colonel FitzGerald to mortal combat for his gross misconduct, and on the 1st October 1797 a hostile meeting took place in Hyde Park; but so dishonourable was the conduct of FitzGerald regarded, that no man of position would act as his second, and thus he was left alone. The combatants exchanged several shots without effect, though placed at only ten paces distant. When the fourth shot from each was discharged, Colonel FitzGerald said he wished to have some advice from Major Wood as a friend.

The major replied, he had no ambition whatever to be regarded as the friend of Colonel FitzGerald, but as a friend of humanity he would desire that Colonel FitzGerald should acknowledge himself the basest of men, and then the duel might close. This Colonel FitzGerald declined, but said he was willing to admit he had acted wrong.

This was deemed insufficient, and the pistols were again

loaded, and discharged without any effect. When each party had fired six shots ineffectually, and Colonel Fitz-Gerald's ammunition was exhausted, he applied to Major Wood for some powder to enable him to continue the duel. This Major Wood refused, though his principal was willing to accede to the request, so the duel was postponed until the next day. The police, however, prevented it, and it was not in this way the abductor met his fate.

The rebellion in Ireland about this time caused Lord Kingsborough to hasten to Mitchelstown. On his arrival, Mr. Barry, who then was proprietor of the Kingston Arms, the hotel of Mitchelstown, informed his lordship that a very suspicious customer had, for a few days, been staying at the hotel, but on hearing that Lord Kingsborough had arrived, asked for his bill, ordered a post-chaise, and went away.

This statement aroused the curiosity of Lord Kingsborough. He saw the post-boy who returned with the empty chaise, and was told he had driven the gentleman to the inn of Kilworth, where he ordered a bed.

As the distance between Mitchelstown and Kilworth was not more than about six miles, his lordship ordered his carriage, and, accompanied by one of his sons, drove at once across the mountains to Kilworth. The small town was shrouded in the gloom of the October evening as the equipage of Lord Kingsborough drew up at the inn, then kept by Mr. Simmons.

To his lordship's inquiry, "Where was the stranger?" was given the answer that the gentleman, on arriving, had dinner, and then went to his bedroom, where he then was.

His lordship bade the waiter tell the gentleman Lord Kingsborough wished to see him for a moment.

The house was small, and the reply was heard by the anxious pursuers. It was, "Go away, I'm in bed, and bring me no messages at this hour."

The tone of the voice confirmed Lord Kingsborough's suspicions as to who was the speaker. He resolved to make certain, and, pistol in hand, went to the bedroom indicated by the voice. The door was locked, but a resolute push from his lordship's shoulder made short work of the barrier, and the party entered the small chamber. The occupant of the bed sprang to the floor, and revealed the vile ingrate Colonel FitzGerald with a pistol in each hand. Before he could use either, the ball from the outraged father's weapon entered his breast, and he fell mortally wounded. Dr. Pigot, the principal physician of the town (father of the late Right Hon. D. R. Pigot, chief baron of the Irish Court of Exchequer), was sent for, but before he arrived the patient was beyond the leech's skill; he was dead. Lord Kingsborough went at once to the nearest magistrate—this was the Earl of Mount-Cashel, whose daughter was the wife of Lord Kingsborough's eldest son—and surrendered himself to abide the result of his act.

A few weeks later, the death of his father, on the 13th November 1797, made him succeed to the title as Earl of Kingston, and, as such, was not amenable to be tried by the going judges of Assize, though there was some question as to the killing of Colonel FitzGerald having occurred before his accession to the title, it did not affect his right to be tried by the more exalted tribunal. It was, however, decided his lordship had his right to be tried by his peers, and this led to the solemn trial in the Irish Parliament House, College Green, Dublin.

The trial took place on the 8th May 1798. The House of Lords did not afford accommodation sufficient for the array of peers and counsel, with all who were required to attend this important trial, so it was found necessary to have the House of Commons fitted up as the Court on this occasion.

This grand apartment was fitted up for the trial. One compartment of seats in the body of the House was appropriated to peeresses, who ranged themselves according to the table of precedence. The members of the Commons and their families also had seats. The Speaker's chair was occupied by the Earl of Clare, lord chancellor, who was lord high steward for the trial. The peers, two marquises—Waterford and Drogheda—twenty-seven earls, fourteen viscounts, three archbishops—Armagh, Cashel, and Tuam—fourteen bishops, and fourteen barons, attended the trial. The peers were in their robes; and the lord high steward and peers being seated,. Sir Chichester Fostescue, king-at-arms, in his official robes, entered carrying the shield with the heraldic blazon of the accused peer. He placed himself on the left of the bar. Next came the Earl of Kingston in deep mourning, and was placed next the king-at-arms. The executioner came next, bearing a large axe. He stood next the prisoner, with the axe held as high as the neck of the accused, but with the blade averted during the trial. It would be turned if the verdict was guilty.

At the Spring Assizes for the county of Cork, in which county the earl had shot Colonel FitzGerald, a bill of indictment having been found by the Grand Jury and transferred to the House of Lords for trial, was then read.

The lord high steward, addressing the prisoner, said: "Robert, Earl of Kingston, you are brought here to answer one of the most solemn charges that can be made against any man, the murder of a fellow-subject. The solemnity and awful appearance of this judicature must naturally discompose and embarrass your lordship. It may, therefore, be important for me to remind you that you are to be tried by the law of a free country, formed for the protection of innocence and the punishment of guilt alone; and it must be a great consideration to you to reflect you are to receive a trial before the superior judicature of the nation, that you are to be tried by your peers, upon whose unbiassed judgment and candour you can have the firmest reliance, more particularly as they are to pass judgment on you under the solemn and inviolate obligation of their honour. It will also be a consolation to you to know that the benignity of our law has distinguished the crime of homicide into different classes. If it arises from accident, from inevitable necessity, or without malice, it does not fall within the crime of murder, and of these distinctions, warranted by evidence, you will be at liberty to take advantage. Before I conclude, I am commanded by the House to inform your lordship and all others who may have occasion to address the Court during the trial, that the address must be to the lords in general, and not to any lord in particular."

The indictment was then again read, and the clerk of the Crown inquired, "How say you, Robert, Earl of Kingston, are you guilty or not guilty of the murder and felony for which you stand arraigned?"

"Not guilty," replied the earl.

To the question, "How he would be tried?" he replied, "By God and my peers."

Then the serjeant-at-arms proclaimed: "Oyez—Oyez —Oyez—All manner of persons who will give evidence upon oath before our sovereign lord the king against Robert, Earl of Kingston, the prisoner at the bar, let them come forth, and they shall be heard, for he now stands at the bar upon his deliverance."

Sir Jonah Barrington, who was present, states: "It is not easy to describe the anxiety and suspense evinced as each witness's name was called over. The eyes of everybody were directed to the bar where the witnesses must enter, and every little movement of the persons who thronged it was held to be intended to make room for some accuser."

No witnesses having appeared, Mr. Curran, who was retained for the defence, had no opportunity for displaying his masterly skill in cross-examination, or his matchless eloquence. The lord high steward then proceeded to ask the important question of each peer, and each according to his rank arose, and, walking past the chair on which the lord high steward sat, placed his hand solemnly on his heart, and said, "Not guilty, upon my honour."

The bishops were not called, as they do not vote in criminal cases.

When all had passed, the lord high steward declared the opinion of the peers was "That Robert, Earl of

Kingston, was not guilty of the charge preferred against him."

Having broken his wand of office, the lord high steward descended from the chair, and the trial was then concluded.

APPENDIX X.

Irish Parliamentary Wits and Humorists.

We may readily believe that an assemblage of three hundred Irishmen, no matter of what rank or avocation, must contain many amusing individuals, and, luckily, one who himself had a reputation perhaps not much to be commended, has very graphically sketched several of his contemporaries.

Of these the most remarkable was Sir Boyle Roche, whose name is identified with the south of Ireland, Boyle being the family name of the Earl of Cork and Earl of Shannon, and Roche, Lord Fermoy. Sir Boyle was representative of many localities during the existence of the Irish Parliament.

Sir Boyle Roche was returned for several Irish boroughs in succession. I find he had been member for Tralee, Portarlington, and Loughlin. He was a sort of whip for the Government, and held some appointment in the Revenue. In discussing a Bill before the House, relating to weights and measures, he expressed his opinion "that every quart bottle should hold a quart." In concluding a speech, he expressed his willingness "to surrender not only a part, but the whole of the constitution, in order to *save the remainder.*" He was a staunch supporter of the Union, and managed to secure for himself and his wife a pension of £500 a year. As the rev. historian of Cork says, "He made no blunder here."[1]

Sir Boyle Roche's most generally known blunder was when, excusing his absence from the House, he assured

[1] Gibson's *History of Cork*, vol. ii. p. 288.

honourable members "that no *man* could be in two places at once, barring *he was a bird*."

Some reference being made to a measure which, if carried, would benefit posterity, was opposed by Sir Boyle, because posterity never did anything for him. It is said he professed to bring in a Bill "that every man should be his own washer-woman."

Another parliamentary humorist, though not a perpetrator of bulls like Sir Boyle Roche, was John Toler, afterwards Chief Justice of the Court of Common Pleas, and a peer with the title of Lord Norbury. He was born at Beechwood, in the county of Tipperary, on 3rd December 1745. It is related that, when dying, his father told him, as his elder brother would inherit the family estate, he could only afford to leave him fifty pounds and these, said the dying Tipperary squire, drawing from beneath his pillow a brace of silver-mounted pistols. "Now, Jack," he added, "with these be always ready to keep up the credit of the family and the character of an Irish gentleman."[1]

Acting on this parental advice, John Toler, both at the Bar and in Parliament, was noted for his duels as readily as in a debate. This was not an unusual mode of argument in the Irish House of Commons. Sir Jonah Barrington having, in the course of an attack on Toler when he was attorney-general in 1797, said the attorney was one of those men who had a hand for everybody, but a heart for nobody. The attorney-general regarded this as an insult, and instantly sent a brother member to demand "an apology, or the usual satisfaction." Sir Jonah was quite willing to give the right hon. gentleman any amount of satisfaction, but no apology; so a meeting was arranged so openly that the Speaker required the serjeant-at-arms to arrest both the belligerents. They sought to evade arrest by means of escape. Barrington got out of the House, but was arrested in Nassau Street, and Toler got outside the door, but shut it so hastily it caught the skirt of his coat, which held him until he was

[1] *The Irish Bar*, p. 112.

arrested. When brought before the Speaker, with his skirts torn off, Curran said, "For one honourable member to trim another's jacket in that fashion, and in the very presence of the Speaker, was quite unparliamentary." The intended duellists, having made apologies, and promising to keep the peace, were then discharged from arrest.

Norburiana.

Some of his legal puns deserve a place in my pages. He and another wit named Parsons were constantly indulging in repartee. One day, while on circuit, the decorous silence of the Court was disturbed by the braying of an ass grazing in a neighbouring field.

"Mr. Parsons," asked the chief justice, "can you make out what noise that is?"

"Merely the echo of the Court," was the caustic reply.

The chief soon paid the wit back. While Parsons was addressing the jury, the ass again began to bray.

"Oh, Mr. Parsons!" said Lord Norbury with a chuckle, "one at a time, if you please."

Notwithstanding these retorts, they were great friends. As both were passing the gaol of Naas in the judge's carriage, observing the vacant gibbet, Lord Norbury said, "Parsons, where would you be if that gallows had its due?" Parsons' retort was ready and deserved. "Riding alone," was the response.

The late Baron Green told me the following anecdote of Lord Norbury:—While trying an action for breach of promise of marriage, some of the letters of the fickle defendant, produced to prove the contract, had been so often shown by the lady to her friends, they were quite frayed, and almost so worn as to be held together with difficulty. Holding one on the palm of his hand when addressing the jury, his lordship said, "Gentlemen, it is easy to see these are love letters, because they are so *mighty tender.*"

An action was brought before Lord Norbury by the son of Lord Waterpark, against the Hope Insurance

Company, to recover a very large sum, for which a villa near Clontarf, County Dublin, had been insured, and which was burnt. The company successfully resisted the claim, as the burning was certainly not accidental.

The plaintiff, shortly after, meeting the chief justice at a levee in Dublin Castle, said, "We meet under different circumstances from our last meeting, my lord. I came here as I intend to present my bride, the Hon. Mrs. Cavendish, at the drawing-room to-morrow night."

"Quite right, sir," replied the chief justice, "the Scripture says, ''Tis better to marry than burn.'"

This judge, whose family name was Toler, was not only witty himself, but the cause of wit in others. I am indebted to Sir Patrick Keenan, resident commissioner of national education in Ireland, for the following epitaph on the deceased lord chief justice :—

> "He's gone, alas! facetious punster,
> Whose jokes made learned wigs with fun stir.
> From Heaven's high court a tipstaff's sent,
> To call him to his punishment;
> Assemble quick, ye sextons ring,
> Let all your clappers ding-dong-ding,
> *Nor bury* him without his due,
> He was himself a *Toler* too."

APPENDIX XI.

Tottenham in his Boots.

We have mentioned that it was customary for the members of the Irish House of Commons to present themselves in the House in Court dress, and those who had orders, stars, etc., wore them. However, there is no general rule without an exception, and that this rule was infringed upon is thus stated by Sir Jonah Barrington.[1]

"A very important constitutional question was debated between the Government and the Opposition, namely, the

[1] *Personal Sketches*, p. 103.

application of a sum of £60,000, then lying *unappropriated* in the Irish treasury, being a balance after paying all debts and demands upon the country and its establishments. The members seemed to be nearly poised, although it had been supposed that the majority would incline to give it to the king, whilst the Opposition would recommend laying it out upon the country, when the serjeant-at-arms reported that a member wanted to force his way into the House, *undressed*, in dirty boots, and splashed to his shoulders.

"The Speaker could not oppose custom to privilege, and was necessitated to admit him. He proved to be Mr. Tottenham of Balycurry, County Wexford, covered with mud, and wearing a pair of huge jack-boots. Having heard that the division was to come on sooner than he expected, he had, lest he should not be in time, mounted his horse at Ballycurry, set out in the night, and ridden nearly sixty miles up to the Parliament House direct, and sought admittance to vote *for the country*. He arrived at the critical moment, and critical it was, for the members being equal, his vote gave the majority of *one* to the country party."

This anecdote is well recollected among the traditions of the Irish senate, and "Tottenham in his boots" was, for a long time, a patriotic toast in the convival banquets of Irish nationalists.

APPENDIX XII.

A very absent Member.

Before the passing of the Octennial Act, the Parliament usually lasted during the life of the sovereign, and as this was sometimes a considerable period, it was a matter of convenience for the members, who took little or no interest in politics, to attend when they felt inclined, or their presence in Dublin during the session enabled them to look in if any interesting matters were to be discussed.

One day a gentleman, who had seldom visited the House of Commons, was proceeding to enter, when he was asked by the door-keeper what he wanted.

"To go to the House," was the reply.

"Have you an order of admission?"

"Oh, I'm a member," said the absentee.

"Where for?" demanded the janitor.

"Faith, I forget the name of the place," replied the member, "but if you have a Watson's Almanack I'll show you;" and so he did.

APPENDIX XIII.

Mr. Pitt's Projects—Disagreement between Parliament.

The learned author of the *Historical Review of the Irish Legislative System* has pointed out that, while the constitution of 1782 made the Irish Parliament perfectly free and independent of that of Great Britain, no provision had been made in case of disagreement in policy between the Parliaments of Great Britain and Ireland. Both were equal, without any controlling authority. No matter how injurious the Irish Bill might be to British interests, the only check was the power of refusing to give the authority of the Great Seal of Great Britain and the royal assent in Ireland.[1] The learned authority states these checks would only apply to Bills and not to resolutions.[2]

The Duke of Portland foresaw the danger of diversity between the two Parliaments, and to obviate the difficulty suggested that in such case control should be given to the Parliament of Great Britain. This was, of course, rendering the Irish inferior to the British Parliament, and therefore the duke's suggestion was not adopted. Some other mode will be more acceptable.

[1] *Historical Review*, p. 138.   [2] *Ibid.* No. BB. p. 278.

INDEX.

À Becket, St. Thomas, 1.
Absentee, Act relating to, 55.
Absentee Act, 26 ; case of, 26.
Acts of William III., 74, 75.
Addison, Joseph, anecdote of, 69.
Adventurers, English, Act, 60.
Alan, Lord Chancellor, 23.
—— Philip, 159.
Anglo-Norman colony, 1.
Anne, Queen, 57, 72, 74, 79.
Anti-Union riot, 64.
Aragon, Catherine of, 27.
Archbold, Thomas, 16.

Ball, Right Hon. J. T., 6, *Hist. Review.*
Barrington, Sir Jonah, 142, 181.
Bedford, Duke of, 81.
Bentinck, Lord George, 137.
Bolton Treatise, 39, 43, 45.
—— impeached, 45.
Bouvet, Admiral, 158.
Boyle, Bishop, 48, 60, 61.
Brodrick, Right Hon. A., 70, 71, 72.
Brown, Archbishop, 22, 44, 45, 73.
Buckingham, Villiers, Duke of, 43.
—— Duke of, 142, 152.
Burgh, Walter Hussey, memoir of, 128.

Burgundy, Duchess of, 17.
Burleigh, Lord, 31.
Butler, Lord J., 24.

Camden, Marquis, 157, 164, 167.
Capel, Lord, 67.
Carteret, Lord, 74, 167.
Castlebar, French at, 167.
Castlereagh, Lord, 163, 197.
Caulfield, Serjeant, 70.
Caxton, W., 13.
Charlemont, Lord, 160.
Charles I., 43, 44, 47, 48, 59, 61.
—— II., 49.
Clare, Earl of, 146. *See* Fitz-Gibbon.
Clarendon, Lord, 49, 171, 173.
Cobbe, Dean, 16.
Coke, Lord, 20, 26.
Cole, Dr., anecdote of, 29.
Connolly, Mr., 153.
Conway, Lord, 61.
Cornwallis, Marquis, 149, 161, 164, 177 ; important dialogues with Mr. Howard, 165, 170, 171, 172, 177.
Corry, Mr., 116.
Cox, Mr., 51, 66, 71.
Cromwell, Lord, 22, 24.
—— Oliver, 42, 47, 48.
—— Richard, 48.
Curran, 142.

Cusack, Thomas, 24.
Cutts, Lord, 66, 67.

DARCY, Patrick, 39.
Davis, Sir John, 41.
—— Thomas, 77.
Derry, Bishop of, 44.
Desmond, Earl of, sad fate, 10; forfeited estates of, 30, 32.
Dublin Castle, 4.
Duffy, Sir C. G., 56, note.
Dungannon Convention, 108.
Duquery, 145.

EDWARD III., 4.
—— IV., 9, 10.
—— VI., 8, 13, 27, 28.
Elizabeth, Queen, 30, 32, 34; her urgent letters to Archbishop Loftus, 35, 36; her clemency, 40, 44, 58.
Emly, Bishop of, 4.
Essex, Earl of, 30.
Eustace, Sir M., 43, 48.
Everard, Sir John, 41.

FITTON, Lord Gawsworth, 50.
FitzEustace, 11.
FitzGerald, Lord Chancellor, 17.
—— Lord Edward, 147.
FitzGibbon (Earl of Clare), patriotic speech when Attorney-General in the Irish House of Commons, important in reference to Home Rule, 147.
FitzHerbert, Mr., 153.
Fitzpatrick, W. J., 147.
FitzWilliam, Earl, 141, 143, 146, 147, 148, 157, 158.
Flood, Henry, memoir of, 104.
Foster, Speaker, 163, 197.
Fox, C. J., 152.
French invasion in Bantry Bay, 158.
—— in Killala, 167.

GEORGE I., Statute 8 Geo. I., 72, 74.
—— II., 65.
—— III., 89; insanity of, 152, 160.
Gilbert, J. T., 8, 15, 16.
Gore, Sir Ralph, 74.
Grafton, Duke of, 76.
Grattan, Henry, memoir of, 113, 141, 143, 144, 145, 155.
Grey, Lord, 15.
—— Lord Leonard, 23.
Grouchy, General, 158.

HENNESSEY, Sir J. Pope, 31.
Henry II., in Ireland, 2; officials, 3; how he became popular, 3.
—— III., 5.
—— VI., 12.
—— VII., 18, 19, 40.
—— VIII., 22, 25, 26, 28, 34, 36; Statute, 66, 67, 68.
Hoche, General, 158.
Howard of Corby, important dialogue with Lord Cornwallis, 165.
Humbert, General, 167.

IRISH industry restricted, 48, 74; how to promote, 75.

JAMES I., confiscation of Ulster, 40, 43, 44, 50, 56, 63; opens Parliament in Dublin, 31–33, 50, 54.
Jennings, Mr., quoted, 34.
John, King, Council of, 3.
Johnson, Dr. Samuel, warning against a Union, Preface, vii., 97.

KEATING, James, 15.
—— Chief Justice, 55.
Keogh, John, 143.
Kildare, Earl of, 11, 14, 15, 16, 17.
Kilkenny, Statute of, 8.
—— confederation of, 47.
King, Archbishop, 52, 53.

INDEX.

LAKE, General Lord, 167.
Langishe, Sir H., 150.
Latouche, J. Digges, 93.
Lecky, Mr., 57, note.
Leland, 29.
Leslie, General, 83.
Lincoln, Earl of, 17.
Loftus, Archbishop, 37.
Lovel, Lord, 17.
Lowther, Sir G., 42.
Lucas, Dr. Charles, memoir of, 90.
Lynch, Mr., 57.

MACMORROUGH, Dermot, 1, 2.
Maddon, D. O., 65.
—— Dr. R. R., 147.
Malone, Right Hon. A., 86.
Mary, Queen, 28, 30, 34.
Mervyn, Sir A., 49.
Molyneaux, William, 60.
Montesquieu, 160.
Montgomery, Lord, 40.
Mountgarett, 63.
Moylan, Bishop, 159.

NAGLE, Sir Richard, 53.

O'BRIEN of Thomond, 3.
O'Connell, Daniel, 105, 175.
O'Donnell, motion by, 169.
O'Neals, 3, 24.
O'Neill, Owen Roe, 47, 48.
Ormonde, Duke of, 52, 54, 67.
O'Rourke, Tiernan, 1.
Oxford, Earl of, 12.

PALE, counties of the, 3.
Pallium, on whom conferred, 28.
Parnell, Mr., 173.
—— Sir John, 144.
Parsons, 145.
Paul VI., Pope, 28.
Peel (1st), Sir Robert, 73.
—— (2nd), Sir Robert, 73.
Pelham, 155.
Pembroke, Strongbow, Earl of, 2, 59.

Perrot, Sir John, 36, 37, 38.
Pery, Speaker, 85.
Phipps, Sir C., 72.
Pitt, Right Hon. Mr., 141, 142, 144, 146, 147, 148, 149, 151, 155, 156, 160, 161, 164.
Plunket, W. C., 161.
Pole, Cardinal, 28.
Ponsonby, Right Hon. G., 144, 145, 153.
Porter, Lord Chancellor, 51, 64, 67.
Portland, Duke of, 143.
Poynings, Sir E., 20, 21.
—— Law, 36, 88.
Protest against the Union, Lords', 175.
Puckering, Sir J., 37.
Pym threat, 46.

RALEIGH, Sir Walter, 30; home at Youghal, 31.
Regency requisite in 1789, 144.
Rigby, Secretary, 81, 85, 86, 87, 88.
Riot, Anti-Union in Dublin, 85.
Rochfort, Speaker, 64.
Ross, General, 166.
Rutland, Duke of, 150, 151.

SHERIDAN, R. B., 128.
Shrewsbury, Earl of, 26, 34.
—— Duke of, 71.
Simnel, Thomas, 18.
Spencer, Edmund, 31, 32.
Strafford, Earl of, 32, 42, 44, 45, 46, 52, 67.
Strongbow, Earl of Pembroke, 2.
Swartz, Martin, 17.
Swift, Dean, 75, 76, 88, 89.
Sydney, Lord, 58.

TEW, Lord Mayor, 85.
Thomond, Earl of, 82.
Tighe, Mr., 169.
Toler, 142; anecdotes of Norburiana, 201.

Tone, Wolfe, 143, 158.
Tottenham, anecdote of, 33.
Tyrconnel, Duke of, 50.

UNION with Great Britain proposed, 141.
—— efforts to promote, 144–146.
—— debate in Parliament, 155, 156.
—— in the House of Lords, 199.
—— Bill passed, 199.

VAUGHAN, Cardinal, 29.

WANDESFORD, Lord Justice, 67.
Waters, 76, 77.

Wentworth, Earl of Strafford, 44.
Westmoreland, Earl of, 142.
Weston, Dr., 35.
Wharton, Earl of, 70.
Whiteside, Chief Justice, 21, 34, 55, 56.
Whitshed, Chief Justice, 76.
William III., 55, 63, 80.
Wilmot, Sir R., 85.
Wogan, Sir John, 6.
Wolfe, 142.
Wood's coinage, 76.
Woodville, Elizabeth, 10.
Worcester, Earl of, 14, 33.
Wraxall, Sir N., 53.

YORK, Richard, Duke of, 7, 8.

APPENDICES.

I. The Irish Parliament Houses, 179.
II. Parliamentary Banquets, 181.
III. Ceremony on opening Parliament, 183.
IV. Procedure of Sessions, 184.
V. Statute Rolls and Journals, 186.
VI. Insults to Statue of William, 187.
VII. Troubles of Speakers, 188.
VIII. Violent Language, 190.
IX. The Kingston Tragedy—tried by his Peers, 191.
X. Irish Parliamentary Humorists, 199.
XI. Anecdote of Tottenham in his Boots, 202.
XII. A very absent Member, 203.
XIII. Mr. Pitt's Projects, 204.

www.ingramcontent.com/pod-product-compliance
Lightning Source LLC
Chambersburg PA
CBHW021841230426
43669CB00008B/1039